Psychosocial Analysis of the Pandemic and Its Aftermath

Psychosocial Analysis of the Pandemic and Its Aftermath

Hoping for a Magical Undoing

Bruno Boccara

HAMILTON BOOKS
AN IMPRINT OF
ROWMAN & LITTLEFIELD
Lanham • Boulder • New York • London

Published by Hamilton Books
An imprint of The Rowman & Littlefield Publishing Group, Inc.
4501 Forbes Boulevard, Suite 200, Lanham, Maryland 20706
www.rowman.com

86-90 Paul Street, London EC2A 4NE, United Kingdom

British Library Cataloguing in Publication Information Available

Library of Congress Cataloging-in-Publication Data

Names: Boccara, Bruno, author.
Title: Psychosocial analysis of the pandemic and its aftermath : hoping for a magical undoing / Bruno Boccara.
Description: Lanham : Hamilton Books, [2023] | Includes bibliographical references and index. | Summary: "Boccara analyzes the Covid-19 pandemic by focusing on the large group unconscious defenses that were mobilized against the anxieties that the pandemic created. He, in turn, argues that humanity will only be able to successfully manage future systemic crises if public policies and country dialogue systematically take into account the underlying psychosocial dynamics"—Provided by publisher.
Identifiers: LCCN 2022035852 (print) | LCCN 2022035853 (ebook) | ISBN 9780761873563 (paperback) | ISBN 9780761873570 (epub)
Subjects: LCSH: COVID-19 (Disease)—Psychological aspects. | COVID-19 (Disease)—Social aspects. | COVID-19 Pandemic, 2020—Government policy | Medical policy. | Crisis management.
Classification: LCC RA644.C67 B627 2023 (print) | LCC RA644.C67 (ebook) | DDC 362.1962/414—dc23/eng/20220802
LC record available at https://lccn.loc.gov/2022035852
LC ebook record available at https://lccn.loc.gov/2022035853

There comes a time when ideas potentially capable of profoundly changing the world must be brought to the centers of decision making. That time is now upon us.

Contents

Acknowledgments

This book was written for its most part during the height of the pandemic, hence during times where most of us found themselves far more isolated than what would normally have been the case. Yet, I would like to acknowledge the significant impact that several individuals had on my reflections leading to the publication of this book.

As always, my thought process owes a great deal to Susan Long and to Vamik Volkan, two authors that have had a major influence on my thinking, creativity and development of my ideas applying psychoanalysis to societies. I also owe a profound gratitude to David Scharff. My most sincere and deeply felt appreciation for everything you have transmitted to me.

In Colombia, I would like to particularly thank Guillermo Calvo Mahé whose continued interest in my work provided a strong motivation to develop the ideas embedded in the book. Guillermo provided critical feedback on the book. In Australia, Susan Long gave me crucial guidance towards structuring and editing the book. In the UAE and the United States, I would like to thank Matthew Hogan whose interest in the book and its relevance towards creating a better world for his now coming of age generation gives me the motivation to continue exploring and applying the ideas on behalf of that generation. In Morocco, I would like to thank Hicham El Habti whose earlier interest and feedback provided the impetus to write this book.

Preface

An essential aim of this book is to advocate for a systematic and embedded psychosocial and systems dynamics approach to public policy and country dialogue. Without this, countries, and indeed any global initiatives to face threats to humanity, will continue to be plagued by destructive, unconsciously held viewpoints, biases, ill-informed prejudices and defensive dynamics that get played out, and rationalized as consciously held policies that often become ultimately destructive. The approach adopted throughout this book, that calls for a worldwide psychosocial renewal, is that of a psychosocial analysis from a systems dynamics (or general equilibrium) perspective. This implies taking into account both societal level unconscious and conscious dynamics. See, Armstrong and Rustin (2004). These dynamics include:

1. Mental representations of various groups in a society;
2. Unconscious fantasies (wishes, perceptions of others and/or of the society, including its cultural heritage);
3. Psychosocial shocks that may impact a society (a pandemic would be one of those);
4. Anxieties, and more generally the psychosocial environment in which societal interactions between various groups take place; and
5. Collective defenses, known as social defenses, mobilized by various groups in response to the anxieties.

This conveys the sense in which the word psychosocial is used. The approach behind the thinking underpinning this book builds upon the rich experience and theory of systems dynamics applied to organizations; a vibrant field of study that owes its theoretical underpinnings to British Object Relations Theory. See, Long (2013) and Scharff (1996). What follows builds directly upon Socio-Analytic Dialogue, an extension and adaptation to countries and their public policies of psychosocial and systems dynamics thinking. See, Boccara (2014).

INTRODUCTION

The arguments and call to action here are motivated by the daunting psychosocial issues that were so strikingly revealed by the Covid-19 pandemic. As argued in the May 2021 UN report prepared by the Independent Panel for Pandemic Preparedness and Response, a series of failures led to the biggest health, social, and economic disaster in living memory. Of particular interest to the thesis of this book is the report's decision to highlight psychosocial issues, in particular the collective denial of facts, which resulted in public policy mistakes and fostered distrust. The denial of the severity of the pandemic has already led to catastrophic outcomes and the worse might yet be to come. In hindsight, much could have been prevented. The book argues that psychosocial dynamics surprisingly strengthened societal denial when the more dangerous delta variant emerged and the situation worsened further once the more contagious omicron variant became dominant. Despite this increase in contagion, several countries drastically altered their public health policies and decided to "live with the virus." Deliberately choosing endemicity of the coronavirus may lead to insurmountable challenges due to the expected continued apparition of new variants for which there would be no immunity. As argued by Bergholtz, Brusselaers, and Ewing (2022), "Just like the process of climate change, COVID-19 also has tipping points . . . The global mutation rate is dependent on the number of infections, and more infections result in more virus replication . . . and is likely to push us . . . to a point beyond which the situation becomes qualitatively irreversible."

As such, humanity is truly finding itself at a turning point. Such an inflexion point in history is likely to be fraught with nearly insurmountable anxieties, hence complex psychosocial dynamics. Facing the extraordinary challenges ahead will require thoroughly and rigorously addressing such psychosocial dynamics—particularly those operating at the societal unconscious level—through the formulation and implementation of psychosocially informed public policy responses and societal level dialogue initiatives. Failing to do this could lead to further psychosocial tipping points. Left unaddressed, the latter could tip the balance in favor a "psychosocial extinction," whereas the world as whole—as a social system defined by its set of collective, or social, defenses—would increasingly mobilize regressed defenses that would make it impossible for societies to manage such challenges. This can be understood as the extinction of good societal thinking in the sense that constructive psychosocial processes would increasingly be replaced by damaging ones.

The pandemic occurred at a time when the world was already facing a daunting psychosocial environment, as evidenced by the increased propensity worldwide for the mobilization of increasingly regressed social defenses. The latter were exacerbated by extreme weather events perceived by the majority as further evidence of climate change (e.g., heat waves in Western North America in 2021, in India in 2022 and floods in Europe in 2021), widening economic disparities, racial and religious animosities and political tensions between many groups both within and between countries. This book argues that such a psychosocial landscape significantly hampered the world's capacity to mobilize in solidarity against the pandemic. This was also often the case within countries.

As such, this book argues that there has probably never been a more critical time than now to genuinely incorporate psychosocial and systems dynamics thinking into public policy and country dialogue; an initiative that would need to continue in the aftermath of the Covid-19 pandemic. This means incorporating an understanding of how mental representations and fantasies, shared anxieties, and social defenses mobilized against those anxieties impact the society. In other words, understanding how nations and the world as a whole function as social systems. Furthermore, this book suggests that humanity's crisis of meaning, fostered by what it considers to be an unprecedented state of acute psychosocial stress, urgently requires psychosocial and systems dynamics thinking to become entrenched rather than only sporadically limited to specific instances or policies. This, in turn, would allow societies to rekindle shared meaning; a prerequisite to their aliveness[1] and ability to confront future crises.

As the book highlights, the core psychosocial response to the pandemic observed in most countries turned out to be a wish for and, in response, enactments of undoing it effortlessly. Wishing it either to magically go away, as if it had never happened or wishing it could be dealt with in an effortless way. Therefore, magical thinking and, as a consequence denial of reality, often prevailed. The lack of capacity of members of most societies to genuinely identify with one another meant that collective efforts to face the pandemic, a la "we are all in this together," were mostly shunned.

The brief description above of the psychosocial landscape in which the pandemic struck certainly seems frightening. Nevertheless, the pandemic is probably not nearly as overwhelming in comparison to what future systemic crises might bring; think of the global extinction threats that humanity seems increasingly likely to face. While this may not suggest a particularly hopeful situation, I believe that hope can exists if we choose to embark on a collective journey of renewal by squarely facing the psychosocial issues that the pandemic has revealed. This does not have to be overwhelming, quite the contrary. The specificity of psychosocial and systems dynamics thinking at the societal level is that, by design, it essentially excludes assigning blame to any particular group. In fact, from the perspective of societal level psychoanalytic inspired thinking that focuses on shared anxieties and unconscious collusions between various subgroups, we automatically position ourselves in an environment in which one can truly say that "we are all in this together." Note that the book often uses "we" with the purpose of inciting the readers to immerse themselves in the book. Working psychosocially on public policy and country dialogue requires people to work together.

The creation of meaning that follows from a society embarking on the collective journey of discovering how it functions as a social system can profoundly alter the way its members interact with one another. The resulting promotion of genuine identification between its members has the potential to allow the society to work through some of the most daunting issues that it may face. Contrary to what would be the norm in public policy or theme-specific country dialogue, this kind of psychosocial initiative would greatly gain in being undertaken while devoid of any specific purpose. This is, in fact, absolutely fundamental. Rather than undertake psychosocial dialogue to confront policy disagreements or cultural differences, one should start the process solely for the sake of the journey itself rather than with specific goals. At its onset, the sole purpose should only be to enable a society to appreciate the complexity and richness of its social system by internalizing the myriad of ways it functions. As such, the psychosocial process would begin by shedding light on the various mental representations, fantasies, social defenses and collusions that make that social system what it is at any given time.

As is well known from the rich literature on the psychoanalysis of organizations, an organization—as a social system—functions both "above" and "below" the surface; the surface being that abstract mental construct separating the societal conscious from the societal unconscious. See, Long (2006).[2] While the psychosocial mechanisms differ when working at the country level, the idea is equally important and applicable. See, Boccara (2014).[3]

In particular, one of the most relevant concepts to understanding country-level psychosocial dynamics, hence its economics and its politics, is perverse societal dynamics. The most important characteristic of perverse societal dynamics relevant to understanding psychosocial issues is the predominance of instrumental relations, whereas most interactions are motivated by narcissistic gratification. It explains why solidarity and collective efforts required to successfully address the pandemic often went missing. In addition, neoliberalism coupled with the internet-fueled revolution has significantly contributed to destroying meaning. This, in turn, significantly complicated most societies' management of the pandemic; the social compacts proving too weak to allow for the solidarity that was required to successively address the pandemic collectively.

Perverse societal dynamics and an increasingly weak capacity for identification, hence lack of empathy, amongst individuals are the key psychosocial attributes that lead us to describe what we are witnessing worldwide as a dangerous slide towards what is symbolically referred to as a "psychosocial extinction." These psychosocial attributes constitute the main impetus for this book's advocating for a systematic and permanent psychosocial and systems dynamics approach to public policy and country dialogue.

Psychosocial and systems dynamics country level approaches require fairly extensive validation to be internalized and, as a consequence, be able to positively and durably impact the psychosocial environment. However, the main purpose of the book is to illustrate concepts to make the case for such interventions. As such, some of the psychosocial dynamics that are identified throughout the book have not always been fully validated. This was neither our purpose and nor was it necessary for the arguments that are made. The book focuses instead on both the psychosocial reasons behind the failure of public health policy responses to reach their objectives and the psychosocial issues that could become substantial obstacles to managing future crises.

There comes a time when ideas potentially capable of profoundly changing the world must be brought to the centers of decision making. That time is now upon us.

ORGANIZATION

The book is organized as follows:

Chapter 1, "And Suddenly, The Future Got Cancelled" introduces the issues and highlights some of the specificities of the pandemic that made it such a formidable event.

The next three chapters are interrelated in the sense that they build directly on Socio-Analytic Dialogue in identifying the purpose and nature of the social defenses that were mobilized against anxieties as well as how leadership responded. Together, a culture of narcissism and declining capacity for identification concomitant with a loss of empathy implied that the pandemic was essentially faced together yet alone. This bodes extremely poorly for future crises and, as such, underscores the urgent need for humanity to rally together to create the shared meaning that is absolutely essential to our collective ability to salvage our future.

Chapter 2, "Socio-Analytic Dialogue in a Time of Pandemic" identifies the key social defenses observed during the early phase of the pandemic before vaccines became available. To do so, it surveys the most salient psychosocial dynamics observed in several countries during that time. It highlights omnipotence, guilt, and atonement; failure foretold; and narcissistic denial.

Chapter 3, "Vaccines and their Vicissitudes" identifies wishing for a magical undoing as the defining psychosocial characteristic that underpinned most of humanity's management of the pandemic. Magical thinking is shown to have reinforced inequality of access to vaccines and led to worsening psychosocial environments in many countries that often ended up choosing to "live with the virus."

Chapter 4, "Leadership and Empathic Capability" surveys how leadership in several countries responded to the social defenses identified in both Chapters 3 and 4 and whether it favored or hindered societal level empathic capability. The latter is identified as playing a key role in enabling countries to successfully manage the pandemic.

Chapter 5, "From Psychosocial Extinction to Psychosocial Renewal" transitions from the pandemic to other systemic crises that humanity is likely to face. As such, it starts with the recognition that today's challenges are on a scale rarely seen before. While this has been resisted in the past, it may now become easier for societies to accept this since the social defenses identified in the book are likely to also be mobilized in similar forms if and when other systemic crises hit. However, psychosocial obstacles to successfully managing future crises include perverse societal dynamics and narcissistic entitlement. The latter is the Achilles' heel currently gripping the world. As such, promoting narcissistic withdrawal is, in our view, one of the most pressing challenges facing humanity.

Chapter 6, "Socio-Analytic Dialogue to the Rescue" introduces Socio-Analytic Dialogue, a psychosocial approach to country-level public policy that would allow the systematic adoption of psychosocial and systems dynamics thinking recommended by the book. It also discusses reparative leadership, which is key to increasing the capacity of a society to effectively contain its members, and psychosocial transmission mechanisms, which determine if and how psychosocial processes succeed in containing societies.

Chapter 7, "If Not Now, When? If Not You, Who?" concludes the book by urging nations worldwide to move forward approaching policymaking, country dialogue and social issues from a psychosocial and systems dynamics perspective.

A Postscript, "Socio-Analytic Dialogue and the Taliban," was added in response to the United States' hasty withdrawal from Afghanistan and the return of the Taliban to power. Similar to what is argued throughout the book for public health policies, the United States' engagement with Afghanistan also reflected its underlying social system. In particular, from a psychosocial perspective, the exit from Afghanistan can also be seen as an elusive search for a magical undoing. Last, along the lines of the book, the postscript argues for genuine identification with the Taliban and others in Afghanistan. It could go a long way towards collective healing.

The Appendix, "Main Theoretical Notions Underpinning Socio-Analytic Dialogue," summarizes the key theoretical aspects, in particular the Socio-Analytic Map of a Country; the two Sequencing Principles; the

Analytical Attitude at the Country Level; and Policies in the Age of Contempt framework.

NOTES

1. Aliveness, a term often used in psychoanalysis, is used here to convey that, similarly to an individual, a society's capable of being sufficiently aware of its internal psychosocial dynamics becomes more vibrant and resilient.

2. Long's seminal work on perverse societal dynamics is crucial to understanding complex psychosocial dynamics at the country level.

3. Boccara's "Socio-Analytic Dialogue" introduced for the very first time theoretical concepts, some adapted from the application of psychosocial and systems dynamics to organizations, and methodology needed to apply that kind of thinking to public policies at the country level.

Chapter 1

And Suddenly, The Future Got Cancelled

IF NOT NOW, WHEN?

While many of us, regardless of where we experienced the Covid-19 pandemic, spent hours dreaming about going back to what once was, the global crisis we are living through might already have changed our world forever. History suggests that pandemics have a significant impact. Thus, how societies managed during the pandemic and the decisions that they will make in its immediate aftermath will likely shape our world for generations to come. Humanity is truly finding itself at a crossroad.

Yet, while the seismic changes we are witnessing may have disruptive consequences, our ability to understand psychosocial issues from a psychosocial and systems dynamics perspective creates a unique opportunity. The time is now upon us to systematically approach our most salient challenges from such a position. Psychosocial dynamics, particularly those whose origins are at the societal unconscious level, matter. They can have a significant impact on policies as well as on ways in which a society experiences and, in turn, responds to those policies. Yet, these psychosocial mechanisms are often misunderstood. This, however, does not imply that they should be ignored. This book reflects on the psychosocial lessons that can be gathered from how various countries are reacting to the pandemic. As such, we ask what can be inferred and learned from the mental representations, anxieties, and social defenses that were, and continue to be observed.

To some, the speed at which medicine was capable of isolating, sequencing and ultimately finding what were portrayed as highly effective vaccines for the new virus was nothing short of amazing; something that will go down in history as one of science and medical research's greatest achievements.

It would be hard, at least from a scientific point of view, to disagree with this. Yet this is nevertheless only valid from an "above" the surface perspective; the surface being that abstract mental construct separating the societal conscious from the societal unconscious. But from a "below" the surface or psychosocial perspective, the story is drastically different. In fact, it is the opposite. This book argues that the social defenses mobilized against the shared anxieties induced by the pandemic point overall towards a catastrophic psychosocial failure. This implies that anxieties, although seemingly reduced at first by the introduction of vaccines, are likely to remain high when the pandemic continues or morphs into variants unable to be contained. Such an outcome, in turn, suggests that the world could well find itself ill prepared to successfully confront future challenges; notably those related to the environment. This is, however, not something that humanity can afford as failure will lead to an ecological disaster. But it does not have to be the case.

By incorporating psychosocial interventions into their policy framework, societies worldwide can increase their resilience and consequently find themselves better prepared to manage forthcoming crises. This requires identifying the nature and psychosocial purpose of the social defenses mobilized. Such identification will act as an input to societies' appreciation of themselves as social systems with potentially destructive unconscious dynamics. This, in turn, creates shared meaning, which enhances the social compact. It also decreases the propensity for those defenses to be regressed and, as such, hamper if not derail public policies.

BRAVE NEW WORLD

Even compared to major conflicts or climate change where, at least for now, geographical areas are neither impacted uniformly nor simultaneously, the Covid-19 pandemic stands out as the very first entirely globalized event; a frightening wakeup call from nature that quickly resonated all over the world. What may have originated in China's Wuhan ended-up reaching all corners of the planet; spreading even to remote Greenland and isolated Pacific territories such as the Marshall Islands and Wallis and Futuna.

History teaches us that a pandemic is likely to have a significant impact on societies worldwide. For example, as Manukyan (2020) argues, the Plague of Justinian challenged traditional beliefs and contributed to the rise of Islam; the Black Death brought the demise of feudalism; smallpox changed the destiny of pre-Colombian America; and the Spanish Flu accelerated the end of World War I while contributing to an increased visibility and changing role for women. While humanity's unparalleled technological advances should have been on track to end the pandemic quickly, the latter has nevertheless laid bare the fragility of our societies and their inability to successfully address global challenges. In particular, the world as a whole was unable to avoid making Covid-19, a virus affecting bats rather than a species closer to man as was the case with HIV, endemic. Global efforts to address the pandemic were hampered by the widespread rejection of what we now see as the necessary steps to stop the disease altogether and the widespread denial of the scientific evidence, in particular that relating to the potential long-term impact of the virus. The initial massive idealization of the vaccines coupled with the huge gains associated with recurrent and mandatory vaccines (or nearly so through the adoption, especially in Europe, of health passes) likely sealed the fate of Covid-19 by significantly decreasing compliance with protective gestures and, as such, ensuring that it would become endemic. As a consequence, our world may have already inexorably changed. Shared anxieties are bound to remain high.

Yet, historical periods of high anxieties are not new. For example, the Industrial Revolution appeared to have been experienced as what Stapley (2006) describes as the "death of a way of life." Experiencing then that something revolutionary was taking place, members of society were drawn to Messianic figures, turned violent or rebelled against authorities. In almost all cases, they experienced a loss of identity. While the seismic changes we seem to be facing now could also bring their share of disruptive consequences, our capacity to understand psychosocial issues from a systems dynamics perspective is something that did not exist before. This creates a unique opportunity. In fact, it is precisely that capacity to make sense and create meaning out of anxiety provoking psychosocial developments, that may allow humanity to successfully navigate the uncharted waters ahead. While searching for meaning during critical times may also not be new, witness Marcus Aurelius, the Roman emperor, writing his Meditations to argue for Stoicism in response to the Antonine plague (another pandemic), the adoption of psychoanalytic-inspired systems dynamics thinking to public policy on a globalized scale would be. But for now, what seemed destined to become a catalyst for tackling global challenges together has, so far, ended-up in a myriad of societal responses that not only often prove to be inadequate but also revealed fragile and poorly understood psychosocial dynamics.

And yet, this book argues that there has probably never been a more appropriate time than the seeming aftermath of the Covid-19 pandemic to genuinely incorporate psychosocial and systems dynamics thinking into the ways that societal members interact and manage their psychosocial environment. A far-reaching crisis requiring urgent and drastic policy responses worldwide may not intuitively appear to be an appropriate time period to do so. Indeed, the pandemic has undoubtedly increased anxieties due to the presence of a highly contagious life-threatening invisible object; an economic downturn that is likely to entail very significant costs; the laying bare of major fault lines in several of the countries impacted by the pandemic; and last but not least, the seemingly widespread feeling, for some possibly unconscious, that the world we once knew will no longer be with us. Nonetheless, the level of anxieties can only be of such magnitude that it has become imperative to genuinely understand ways in which psychosocial environments have been and will continue to be impacted. Not doing so can only worsen the already virulently polarized political climate that is prevalent in many societies.

Incidentally, the high level of shared anxieties surmised above was corroborated by ongoing work in social dreaming regarding the frequency and intensity of Covid-19 related dreams as well as by surveys.[1] As the collective journey of creating our post-pandemic world is just beginning, the time is upon us to incorporate a psychosocial and systems dynamics approach to public policy and country dialogue along the lines argued in Socio-Analytic Dialogue. See, Boccara (2013a) and Boccara (2014). Denying us the opportunity to do so will likely be a costly missed opportunity. Taking into account and working through the psychosocial issues pertaining to the pandemic—an anxiety-provoking event par excellence—will provide meaning and, as a consequence, significantly increase our collective readiness to understand and address it and its aftermath. It will also facilitate societies and governments reflecting upon and generating greater consensus as to what our post Covid-19 world may and should resemble.

NOTES

1. See, "Social Dreaming Matrix," Tavistock Institute, accessed June 1, 2021, https://www.tavinstitute.org/social-dreaming-matrix and "Global Prevalence and burden of anxiety disorders in 204 countries and territories in 2020 due to the Covid-19 pandemic," *The Lancet*, Volume 398, Issue 10312, October 8, 2021.

Chapter 2

Socio-Analytic Dialogue in a Time of Pandemic

As indicated in the preface, this chapter and the one that follows identify the purpose and nature of the social defenses mobilized against anxieties during the pandemic. What follows focuses on the social defenses observed before vaccines became available.

AT THE BEGINNING WAS THE DEED

Interestingly, the global pandemic that emerged in Wuhan, China is now celebrated there as a victory rather than remembered as a tragedy; the inhabitants of the 11 million strong city seemingly all too happy now to glorify the Chinese authorities' successful management of the pandemic. The city even opened an exhibition hall showcasing the all-out war waged by the authorities against Covid-19. Thus, in an undoing par excellence, the "pandemic in the mind" in Wuhan, meaning how it is "chosen to be remembered," appears to have been transformed from a "bad" into a "good" object. This is quite an undertaking given the suffering and toll that the pandemic had there. Furthermore, while Covid-19 was undoubtedly successfully eradicated in that city, restaurants were thriving and markets bustling less than a year after it had implemented the strictest lockdown on January 23, 2020, the authorities and the local population are increasingly embracing the narrative that the pandemic came from abroad (i.e., the Americas) rather than having originated in their own city. In a psychosocially stunning move, the "pandemic in the mind" is, therefore, not only ridden of its "bad" qualities but is also portrayed, meaning how it is "chosen to be experienced," as an object that could not possibly have originated there and, as such, not having possibly emerged from the city's world-renowned laboratory in spite of the latter being specifically dedicated to the study of coronaviruses capable of creating a pandemic.

Although the latter was periodically brought up in the press outside China at the onset of the pandemic, our purpose in what follows is not to argue its veracity but rather to focus on the psychosocial dynamics that often came up whenever that hypothesis was brought up.

While early claims were made that the Covid-19 virus shared sequences with the HIV virus and could, as such, only have been created in a research laboratory and accidentally released, these were quickly rejected by most authorities and populations. The virus itself is generally thought to have evolved in its natural hosts, Covid-19 viral genome sequences reported in bats and pangolins, before infecting humans once spike proteins had mutated and allowed it to infect human cells. This is consistent with what is understood to have been the case with both SARS and MERS. But rather than being evaluated for their merits, claims about the laboratory genesis were so quickly discarded that it is likely that it was psychosocially preferable to immediately ignore them. As is often the case in such situations, there were likely unconscious collusions contributing to this outcome. For example, the World Health Organization (WHO), which was part of a joint study with China to determine the origins of the virus, albeit with data exclusively provided by the Chinese authorities, agreed to a report that gave almost no consideration to that possibility.[1]

The psychosocial environment impacts the speed and intensity with which alternative views get traction or get discarded. While this kind of psychosocial phenomenon ultimately fails to maintain traction whenever something can be rigorously explained hence impossible to deny, this was not necessarily the case with the origins of Covid-19 at the onset of the pandemic. For example, calls for a more thorough investigation, the earlier claims judged sufficiently credible at the time to warrant an investigation, were made in May 2021 by world renowned researchers.[2] In addition, a highly respected French TV program,[3] *Envoyé Spécial* broadcasted by the most recognized French public national television channel basically concluded that the scientific evidence pointed to the Covid-19 virus having emerged from the Wuhan lab with a high probability. According to the broadcast, there were several security lapses; something that had also been flagged in a Washington Post article.[4] Furthermore, several scientists contracted a lethal pneumonia like disease in China after having been exposed to a coronavirus, RaTG13, that originated in bats and whose genome sequence is the closest to that of Covid-19. The scientists interviewed in the French TV program alleged that the Covid-19 virus might have been manipulated, albeit unintentionally and for research purposes. Their views were that the original RaTG13 had its protein spike specifically modified to render it highly capable of infecting humans with the purpose of studying the virus to understand how to protect humans from coronaviruses if and once they mutate. Last, during the last days of the Trump administration, declassified intelligence indicated that Wuhan lab staff had to be hospitalized after experiencing Covid-like symptoms in the fall of 2019 before the outbreak was disclosed. From an "above" the surface perspective, the United States could be reluctant to let this kind of information out since the National Institute of Health (NIH) partly funded the research undertaken in Wuhan. From a "below" the surface perspective, coming to terms with such an idea would probably have to be resisted. Regardless of their validity, beliefs that Covid originated from the lab in Wuhan would feed strongly into mental representations of China as a threatening "bad" object and, as such, lead to unwanted hostilities.

More generally, albeit maybe not applicable here from what is now understood, this kind of hypothesis, similarly to what can happen with a public policy, can often become "hijacked" by social defenses. Hypotheses can become difficult to confront if they go against the existing set of social defenses. Incidentally, had it been established that the virus accidentally leaked out of a research lab, there would not only be risks of an angry backlash but also a withdrawal worldwide from accepting the collective responsibility for the pandemic. This is absolutely fundamental since the collective failure to manage has largely been driven by a failure amongst large segments of the population, if not entire nations, to collectively own to the pandemic as a shared burden. The latter is, however, relevant since an economic way of thinking that is excessively conducive to a perceived encroachment on different species' living environments favors the emergence of viruses jumping from animal species to humans.

Incidentally, it would also be difficult for China to hide for very long the fact that the pandemic had originated in a lab. Shi Zengli, the well-known Chinese scientist and director of the Center for Emerging Infectious Diseases at the Wuhan Institute of Virology, has worked extensively with foreign scientists and, in particular prominent ones from the United States. While potential collusions between nations could make it harder to establish the origins of the pandemic, such collusions would be nearly impossible to maintain since sooner or later, the truth—also known by actors outside China—would likely come out.

China, on the other hand, was probably reluctant to immediately acknowledge the severity and risks of what was unfolding in Wuhan. A trust building psychosocial understanding between the rest of the word, particularly the United States, and China might have allowed on its part an earlier acknowledgement of Covid-19 (rather than end-of-December 2020). Precious weeks were likely lost within China, and for similar psychosocial reasons, outside China. And, what applies to China also applies elsewhere. For example, the immediate disavowal of the seriousness of what was to come by the Trump administration, too eager to talk about the "China virus" as if this in itself would make it disappear, is probably one of the costliest psychosocial health policy responses seen in modern times. But, like the foretold yet systematically denied events that were the hallmark of Greek tragedies, the pandemic soon reached Western Europe and North America. Interestingly, Oedipus the King, the most famous Greek tragedy, premiered during the plague that Athens experienced around 429 BC during the Peloponnesian war; ancient Greeks actually watching Sophocles' play on denial and the incapacity to forestall fate during a pandemic.

The worse was about to unfold.

LOCKDOWNS AND THEIR VICISSITUDES: OMNIPOTENCE, GUILT AND ATONEMENT

The observed psychosocial dynamics as the pandemic reached European shores defied expectations. By April 2020, almost 4 billion people—totaling more than half of the world's population—had now been ordered to stay at home. While some countries only had partial lockdowns (e.g., not all states in Brazil or in the United States), there were only a handful that chose not to impose some forms of stay-at-home orders.[5]

Lockdowns started seemingly effortlessly with the majority of countries adopting strict stay at home orders with little, if any, questioning or resisting. Second, in a startling development, those lockdowns were quickly romanticized rather than dreaded for what the shared sacrifice was likely to entail. While these early reactions may have played a defensive role to facilitate coping, something else was also at play. Confinements were often portrayed as special opportunities, even welcomed gifts, to heal the entire planet.[6] Thus, there were countless social media posts in awe of nature regenerating itself. Yet, while the canals in Venice might have been cleaner in the absence of gigantic cruise ships, there were no dolphins to be seen in spite of what, just to give an example, a tweet with a million likes might have implied. TV stations delighted in showing repeatedly before and after pictures of the India Gate in Delhi that had become so much easier to see following India's lockdown thanks to air pollution diminishing quickly. Individuals delighted in sharing pictures of wild boars roaming the streets of Ajaccio in the French island of Corsica, of pumas in Santiago, Chile, and of a herd of deer in East London. But pictures were also often doctored, as was for example the case in India with pictures of wildlife roaming deserted urban spaces. This suggests that while nature might have indeed regenerated itself to some degree, albeit probably not right away as some pictures suggested, there first and foremost existed desire for such changes, hence the presence of psychosocial needs to see nature regenerating itself.

As underscored by Rosa (2020), what could not be done during years of increasing awareness and concern about overexploitation of earth's resources and by countless world level conferences had just been accomplished in nearly no time at all. The entire world had come to a halt. What had always been assumed to be impossible, viz. stopping the frenetic and unbounded use of resources in the name of the economic growth to which we had become addicted, suddenly became reality. The elusive was now real. The extraordinary nature of what was taking place, included what it implied on public freedom, suggests that beyond the public health rationale for the lockdowns, powerful psychosocial mechanisms must also have been at play. It is, otherwise, hard to conceive that engineering a sudden and coordinated brake on almost all economic activities worldwide, an action that had to be undoubtedly feared for its likely disastrous economic consequences, could have occurred so rapidly across so many different countries.

What follows focuses on what those psychosocial mechanisms might be, starting first with forestalling a loss of omnipotence.

By immediately taking charge of the situation, governments were most likely experienced psychosocially as restoring the omnipotence that felt suddenly lost at the onset of the pandemic. The unbearable anxiety due to losing omnipotence, akin to a psychosocial death foretold, had to be of such magnitude that it would need to be responded to defensively with an undoing aimed at instantly regaining, even if only in fantasy, what had just been lost. Implementing strict measures, systematically eschewing alternatives, is likely to have provided a reassuring sense of control. Thus, few countries chose to even reflect upon the potential validity of less stringent approaches. A well-known exception was Sweden, which maintained decent epidemiologic data for quite some time but, unfortunately, ended-up with a far worse situation that its neighbors; a situation that continued throughout 2021. And yet, the country's chief epidemiologist, Anders Tegnell, consistently advocated, to the dismay of most scientists there, against mask wearing including when the country confronted the far more contagious omicron variant. Furthermore, several countries immediately enacted strict border closures. For example, the three Maghreb countries of Morocco, Algeria, and Tunisia chose to act quickly and drastically by immediately closing all their borders. Notwithstanding that some foreigners were temporarily caught in those countries with no way out, such borders closures suggested the existence of pressing needs to reassess control by rigidly splitting the environment between a safe space inside and a dangerous and persecutory space outside. This splitting of space was also observed in Australia where even nationals faced significant obstacles returning to their home country; an ethically questionable situation that continued for nearly two years and became a major crisis once

Australians found themselves trapped in India at a time when Covid cases and deaths there were rising exponentially.

We now continue our analysis by focusing on the psychosocial dynamics underpinning the idealization of the lockdowns.

It is by now well accepted that uncontrolled—and almost always highly unequal[7]—economic growth is likely leading to irreversible destruction of the environment. As is also well known, biodiversity loss and climate change, whose consequences threaten life support systems, is one of the most serious risks we are collectively facing right now. And yet, these threats, too anxiety provoking to fathom, have been met with several levels of denial. See, Long (2015) and Hoggett, Hollway, Robertson and Weintrobe (2022). These include outright denial (i.e., it does not exist); manic denial (i.e., hubristic beliefs that it can be overcome by technology and, as a consequence that unrestricted economic growth is feasible); and denial of responsibility (i.e., a depressive stance which leads to feelings of powerlessness under the beliefs that ultimately nothing can be done). However, while mobilizing denial defenses against the risks of environmental catastrophes, notwithstanding the significant cost of doing so, had until now remained an option, such tactics could no longer hold once the pandemic hit. This is absolutely fundamental. Catching the world by surprise, too sudden and too raw at its onset, Covid-19's irruption on the collective imagination worldwide succeeded in what until then had been elusive; breaching our omnipotence. It forced us, at least momentarily, to come face to face with our own fragility. In an intense moment of unity, the world came to a standstill. At that point, in displacement and under the form of a virus as an invisible yet lethal object, the unsustainability, perhaps even the immorality, of the ways in which our economic structures dictate our relationship to both the environment and to one another could no longer be reasonably denied.

Losing the ability, even if only temporarily, to successfully mobilize a denial social defense in response to environmental catastrophe is, in our view, what contributed to both the romanticizing of the lockdowns as well as the immediate and near total acceptance of strict measures. The lockdowns, whose feasibility was as a consequence not even remotely questioned, became a tool to address collective guilt as well as anxiety brought about by poor management of the environment. This is precisely why the mental representations of the lockdowns, or "lockdowns in the mind," became so quickly associated with environmental restitution, in other words experienced as collective repair acts. As such, the lockdowns morphed into acts of atonement and of reparation for the damage perpetrated on the planet. They were, therefore, embraced by many rather than resisted. In addition, in its unprecedented collective ability to bring the world economy to a standstill, humanity was psychosocially also aiming to create for itself a convincing narrative that it had the capacity to "do something." Thus, while the lockdowns were justified with the ubiquitous "flattening the curve" argument, the latter could only be one part of the story. From a psychosocial perspective, quickly regaining control of the pandemic not only allowed regaining the omnipotence that had been temporarily lost but also provided an opportunity, until then elusive, to redeem ourselves. The corollary is that whenever lockdowns faltered, anxieties other than those discussed above had to be involved so as to render the continued maintenance of a confinement psychosocially too difficult for a majority of the population.

This is not to say that the epidemiologists' justifications for the lockdowns were not valid (it ensured that medical facilities would not be overstretched and allowed for a decrease in the factor of transmission, R_0[8]) but that their acceptance, hence their ease of implementation at the onset, was greatly facilitated by the fact that the anxiety associated with loss of omnipotence coming from a deadly pandemic and the annihilation anxiety and concomitant guilt associated with climate change were both conveniently defended against. The lockdowns, therefore, I hypothesize, played a defensive role. Those psychosocial benefits, unconscious at least in part, undoubtedly played a significant role in countries choosing and implementing confinement policies.

Marveling at the extraordinary environmental benefits, even if only in fantasy, was therefore not an odd sideshow but rather a fundamental aspect of the confinement policies. It played an essential psychosocial function without which those policies might have been more prone to derailing, especially in light of their harsh impact on the poor in the developing world who live day to day. But this is still not the whole story. Climate change cannot be understood without reference to our economic system and its relentless focus on unbounded exploitation of the earth's resources. As is well known, the costs of our greed-driven insatiable obsession with economic growth have been high. Besides environmental degradation, these costs also include increased pauperization, increasing income inequality, and on the psychosocial front, the destruction of existing social compacts due to a weakening of basic trust. The obscene greed and its economic consequences are in our view what underpin the unacknowledged guilt brought by our mismanagement of the environment. Therefore, with guilt as another prominent psychosocial affect involved in our relationship to the environment, we consider that the pandemic and the self-imposed sacrifices that it entailed were experienced "in the mind" as a required repair act. It provided humanity with an opportunity to redeem itself. Thus, in our view, from a psychosocial and systems dynamics perspective, the initial response to the pandemic became a collective act of atonement. Regardless of whether lockdowns were the only option (given shortages of protective equipment, paucity of available intensive care units, shortage of tests and lack of contact tracing), the extraordinarily punitive measures adopted must also be understood in the psychosocial context that the pandemic created.

But the honeymoon period, i.e., the process whereby most societies found ways to "enthusiastically" embrace the admonished protective gestures to address the pandemic, was all too short-lived. This reversal of sentiment was also exacerbated by situations where poor management led to countries going in and out of lockdowns, France for example, or to unusually extensive lockdowns. Toronto in Canada stands out as the city having put in place one of the longest restrictions; indoor dining—as part of a lockdown that began on April 8, 2020—was still totally restricted more than a year later with the exception of a brief reopening in the summer of 2020. This exceeds the duration of restaurant closures in the hard-hit cities of Paris and Buenos Aires. Seoul, in contrast, never closed its restaurants while the harshest complete lockdown was Melbourne's 110 days, far exceeding Wuhan's 76 days. The situation in Ontario, which was hit hard by a third wave at a time Canada was lagging behind its neighbor to the south on vaccination, highlights the importance of leadership; Ontario's performance turning out to be far worse than that of other provinces, notably the Atlantic ones. We return to the psychosocial aspects of leadership in the next chapter.

Last, in shared grandiose fantasies of restoring omnipotence, most societies failed to sufficiently reflect of the psychosocial costs of what those lockdowns entailed. Rather than include in the public debate those that were vehemently against the lockdowns, the latter's "heretical" voices were automatically shunned and precious psychosocial data, that would have been useful to have at the onset, were lost. In hindsight, the stage was set for an irreversible hardening of positions on both sides of what were to become lockdowns, masks and vaccines. The splitting and denial that ensued greatly contributed to the collective failure to prevent Covid-19 to almost certainly become endemic.

TO MASK OR NOT TO MASK: PSYCHOSOCIAL FAILURE FORETOLD

At the onset of the pandemic, many governments argued that masks were not necessary outside medical settings and strongly discouraged their use. For example, on January 24, 2020, the then French minister of health argued that the probability for the virus to spread from Wuhan to Europe was extremely small. And yet ironically albeit unknown to the authorities at the time, the nation's first three cases were identified that very same day. Two days later, the same minister argued that surgical masks were absolutely useless in preventing propagation. It, however, also quickly became known that surgical masks were extremely scarce while the stock of far more protective N95

(FFP2) masks was essentially non-existent. The government felt that it had no choice but to strongly discourage, even prevent, the public from acquiring masks. The next step was for the health authorities to craft a message denying the usefulness of wearing mask in fighting the pandemic, rationalization used as a defense disguised as a logical necessity, by focusing instead almost exclusively on protective gestures, particularly the disinfecting of hands and surfaces. Once it was revealed that a large number of expired masks that could possibly have been used for the population at large had been destroyed, it became increasingly clear to the population that the French government was purposely not being transparent. And, public trust eroded right from the onset of the pandemic. It was only in April of 2020 that the authorities started to encourage the population to wear masks, medical grade or not, and in August of 2020 that wearing a mask became compulsory in all enclosed public spaces.

As was the case elsewhere, erratic and constantly changing recommendations from governments at a time of high anxieties turned out to be quite costly. The absence of constancy decreased governments' ability to adequately respond to the many defensive needs that existed among the populations in various countries. As is always the case on the psychosocial front, there will always be attempts to defend against collective anxieties by mobilizing a set of social defenses. The notion that psychosocial dynamics can lead to policies being used as defenses is rarely, if ever, taken into account by governing bodies. This is the case because social defenses are different from most psychological aspects traditionally encountered in public policy since they are mostly unconscious and collusive. Furthermore, there are no alternatives as far as anxieties are concerned; they must be alleviated. As such, in what follows, we return to the twin psychosocial pillars underpinning the pandemic: denial and the wish to undo. Although time made it easier to identify the ubiquity of denial and of undoing social defenses, one can be almost certain—the same anxieties had to be there from the very beginning of the pandemic—that these were also the social defenses unconsciously mobilized at the onset. Thus, while governments may have been insufficiently aware of the underlying psychosocial dynamics, their early policy responses were nevertheless interpreted—and responded to—as a function of the defensive needs that existed at the onset of the pandemic. And lack of awareness does not imply, or mean, that unconscious collusions between the general public and the authorities did not exist. In fact, downplaying the seriousness of the pandemic at the onset was also most likely the result of those collusions; the denial fulfilling a psychosocial role for both the authorities and the public. While the early policy responses enabled that denial, it can only have, at best, worked partially. After all, France and other Western countries had access to the same information that was available to nations such as Vietnam and

Thailand where far stricter containment measures were implemented immediately. It is likely that countries that experienced earlier scares (e.g., SARS) were better prepared, including with respect to their collective capacity to work though their anxieties since they had faced similar ones before.

But if denial was, at best, only going to work partially, other social defenses needed to be summoned. What could not be denied had to be undone! Therefore, alleviating anxieties, which incidentally kept increasing in intensity, made it psychosocially essential to mobilize an undoing social defense. With the pandemic still in its infancy, the only option in the absence of other announcements and/or policies was to "hijack" the government's message on protective gestures as a social defense. As a consequence, in spite of initially doubting the validity of focusing almost exclusively on cleaning hands and surfaces (after all doctors do use medical grade masks to protect themselves), disinfecting became almost right away experienced as an undoing ritual. Once this mental representation became anchored, meaning internalized, magical thinking on what was seen as a simple and reassuring solution would make it difficult to change course as far as policies were concerned.

It would have been better for the authorities in France to admit to the masks shortage and encourage instead the population to rally together in an act of solidarity in fabricating and distributing homemade masks. Once availability allowed it, then shifting to masks would likely have been far easier. From a psychosocial perspective, masks would have immediately been experienced as an object capable of enabling the wished-for undoing. As such, they would have been imbued with magical qualities; something that could only have positively impacted populations' compliance with protective gestures. Instead, protection often ended-up being quite low, something that can only have contributed to the country's dismal performance in managing the pandemic.

The foregoing was, of course, not limited to France. In fact, the WHO and the Center for Disease Control (CDC) in the United States had also argued against masks at the onset. Yet the social defenses mobilized were not identical. Similar to what was observed in France, the supply of protective masks was very low in the United States. While the authorities felt that they had no choice but to safeguard masks for health care workers, the general public often reacted to the authorities' discouraging mask wearing by heavily discounting their effectiveness in managing the pandemic. But unlike in France, and essentially everywhere else, mask wearing also quickly became a marker of cultural identity. This is absolutely fundamental because the nature of the social defenses mobilized whenever identity is under attack can be quite regressed. As such, their impact can be quite strong. While this psychosocial aspect is particularly relevant whenever ethnic identity is under attack as can be seen during ethnic based conflicts and resulting acts of ethnic cleansing, it is nevertheless also relevant whenever a society has become split across cultural lines, as has been the case in the United States. As such, mask wearing grew aligned along political affiliations; a much larger share of Republicans, particularly die-hard Trump supporters, rejecting mask wearing not only as an affirmation of their identity but also as an attack from whom they were so keen to differentiate themselves. While President Trump, mocking those that wore masks, encouraged this, splitting along cultural lines in the United States predates Trump's election. In fact, it explains it. Thus, the psychosocial environment was already particularly prone for an object, here protective masks used against the "imported" pandemic (Trump's China virus), to be chosen to mobilize a splitting social defense. As such, anti-masks supporters justified their stance by appropriating for themselves a variety of arguments ranging from feminist ideas on personal choice surrounding the body to fringe conspiracy theories.[9]

Enactments, as is often the case when regressed social defenses are mobilized, are often prone to follow. For example, in Michigan, the state where a plot to kidnap and kill Governor Whitman took place,[10] a security guard at a Family Dollar store in Flint was shot after asking a customer to wear a mask. Tensions between passengers or with flight attendants on US domestic flights quickly became out of hand. The foregoing examples above highlight the importance of keenly understanding the psychosocial environment in which public policies are designed and implemented. Mental representations also impact ways in which those policies are experienced. They impact the likelihood for other issues to be displaced onto those policies and for those policies to be "hijacked" by social defenses. Public policies can appear to be well designed but yet fail because of those psychosocial dynamics that remain unaccounted for. In ignoring psychosocial aspects, public policy responses to the pandemic have almost always been carried out in a vacuum, eliciting resistance to change that was often misdiagnosed. Psychosocial dynamics are capable of explaining otherwise seemingly irrational societal dynamics surrounding policies.

In almost all affluent Western countries, governments failed to assess the impact of mental representations on their management of the pandemic. For example, by introducing complex mask wearing requirements (e.g., mandatory in certain streets of Paris rather than throughout the city), the French authorities induced the population into experiencing mask-wearing as a constraint imposed by the state, hence a burden, rather than as a noble act of solidarity; the latter a message that could resonate particularly well in a country with a high level of social conscience. As discussed in the next section, encouraging mask-wearing as an act of solidarity in the United States, the mask worn first and foremost to protect others rather than oneself, was counterproductive and as such backfired in an extremely individualistic society in which the capacity for identification with other members of the society has likely considerably weakened. Embracing rather than shunning mask-wearing, which has to be the most important protective gesture regardless of vaccination status, would have gone a long way in enabling several European countries to avoid going back and forth between putting in place restrictions and rescinding them. The latter ended up destroying the respective governments' credibility and ultimately made managing the pandemic nearly impossible. For example, in November 2021, Denmark, which had lifted all its pandemic restrictions in September 2021 declaring that Covid-19 was no longer "an illness, which is a critical threat to society," reintroduced its corona pass. In a highly discriminatory move, Austria opted to re-confine its unvaccinated population. And less than two months later, when confronted with the omicron variant, several governments including Israel that had managed so well, decided to let their society "live" with the virus, regardless of what was increasingly known about the long-term consequences of the disease, notably on the brain.

This section also highlights the importance of leadership. While Trump could not singlehandedly impact the way the United States, as a social system, chose to handle the pandemic, he very much had an influence. Yet, the social system, meaning the psychosocial mechanisms underpinning the mobilization of social defenses, always remains the main determinant. Thus, in spite of seemingly large differences between the time Trump was President and the time Biden succeeded him, the way the social system handled the pandemic was nevertheless almost identical.

To this, we now turn.

FACING THE PANDEMIC TOGETHER YET ALONE: NARCISSISTIC DENIAL IN THE USA

This section focuses on the way the pandemic was managed in the United States. Thanks to allocating resources and efforts towards a largely successful vaccine drive, the United States, following a disastrous start, seemed poised to successfully manage the pandemic. This, however, soon faltered. Strong opposition to vaccines coupled with resistance to collective efforts at mitigating the circulation of the virus turned out to be a dangerous combination of psychosocial obstacles.

The last point is particularly relevant. Policymakers can, as they usually ultimately end-up doing, recognize certain risks once they become obvious. However, such risks would almost always be relatively easy to foresee with an ex-ante understanding of the underlying psychosocial dynamics. To do so, however, adds complexity. Such dynamics are likely the result of unconscious collusions of which those policy makers are also part. This is the binding constraint; unconscious aspects left hidden and, as such, "unseen" by those policy makers. Moreover, their conscious effects may be purposely hidden to ideological or other interests.

This only holds until the underlying psychosocial dynamics are elucidated and resistance to accepting them is sufficiently weakened. Thus, the increasingly strong rebound of the pandemic during the summer of 2021 is entirely consistent with enactments surrounding shared wishes to undo the pandemic. The latter, as will be shown, included undoing-driven premature re-openings as well as lifting of all mask mandates. Furthermore, in spite of ample evidence to the contrary from other countries, the United States ignored the dangers of a vaccination campaign running out of steam while more contagious and virulent variants were becoming dominant. Overall, from a purely psychosocial perspective, the United States found itself largely unable to address the pandemic. While individual sacrifices were made, notably by health care professionals who went out of their way to save lives and by businesses that endured significant hardships, the nation, as a social system, could not mobilize the solidarity that was required to successfully manage the pandemic. The fact that this occurred in spite of government support programs, unavailable in poorer countries, that aimed at lessening the economic burden of the pandemic on households (e.g., income support, tax deferrals, eviction moratorium) further underscores this. This greatly matters since the psychosocial dynamics that proved to be nearly insurmountable obstacles this time around are likely to be similar if and when other systemic crises hit.

Regardless of its success, an exclusive reliance on the vaccines bodes poorly for the future. Effortless once it becomes available to the general public, such a technical solution by itself is without the capacity to induce the mettle for collective solidarity and hence is likely to fail. What if vaccines are not that swiftly available? What if vaccines, as looks to be increasingly the case, are not that effective? South Korea illustrates particularly well how this could and should have been managed. In fact, the experience of the United States stands in sharp contrast with that of South Korea, that successfully controlled the pandemic through public health measures whose success showcases the social cohesion and public trust that are the hallmark of this Asian nation.

In contrast with the United States, South Korea was able to set up the largest and best-organized epidemic control program in the world through mass testing the population (at a rate of 700 times that of the United States) particularly at drive-through screening facilities and tracing those with whom infected individuals had been in contact. As such the country did not have to resort to lockdowns. While contact tracing reliant on phone and credit card use and the requirement for infected individuals to go into isolation in government shelters may have raised privacy concerns, the government widely relied on transparent information and public participation. In fact, the current president's approval rating rose during the pandemic while that of his predecessor had sharply fallen during the MERS epidemic widely seen having been poorly managed. And while South Korea had only barely started its vaccination campaign, it was nevertheless still controlling the pandemic extremely well. Not becoming hostage to adverse psychosocial dynamics is what sets South Korea apart from the many countries, mostly western, that struggled to contain it. The contrast between the United States and South Korea highlights the importance of systematically striving to understand the psychosocial context as a way to avoid public policies and sentiment being hijacked as social defenses.

What follows is the unsettling story of a social system's manic-depressive response to a pandemic. While the focus is on the United States, the psychosocial dynamics that are identified and the conclusions are relevant to broader contexts.

The analysis begins with the Center for Disease Control's sudden and totally unexpected decision to "liberate" America from pandemic related restrictions on May 13, 2021. As might be expected, the CDC justified the latter solely on medical grounds, as if there could not also be psychosocial factors behind that decision. And yet, the individuals that enthusiastically embraced the early successes of the US vaccination campaign, incidentally as if the rest of the world did not matter, understood perfectly the risks of an insufficiently high vaccination rate combined with the rise of far more contagious variants. But these individuals, perhaps hostage to a social system, exulting in grandiose fantasies early on, were now, on behalf of the majority of the population, mobilizing to defend their (and that of most) ability to maintain those fantasies. It however turned out to have been premature. Once again, systematic and ongoing analyses of underlying psychosocial dynamics would avoid situations such as these.

Developments in the United States surrounding the management of the Covid-19 pandemic have overall been quite worrisome. While some countries found themselves unprepared and ended up making strategic mistakes (e.g., the UK and its delayed decision to close down following a short-lived attempt at aiming for herd immunity; France and its poor management of protective personal equipment), the United States stood out for its manic depressive like relationship to the virus. Thus, individual states wavered between weakly enforced and poorly respected, seemingly strict lockdowns and economic apertures: opening the space for not wearing a mask to become a symbol of defiance. Violent enactments sometimes followed, as was the case with white nationalists storming the Capitol in Lansing, Michigan in the name of freedom from Covid restrictions. And then as mentioned earlier, all of a sudden with the vaccine drive still ongoing but nowhere near completed enough for the country to consider itself safe from further propagation of the virus, the CDC announced on May 13, 2021, that vaccinated individuals could do away with mask wearing, including indoors. Once again, shared wishes to undo the pandemic had effortlessly been transformed into a reality. Interestingly, Israel, the country always given by the CDC as the example to emulate for its successful vaccination, had decided to maintain a strict mask mandate indoor in spite of lifting most remaining restrictions. But who was to tell who was vaccinated and who was not? What could possibly go wrong? In fact, the grocery chain Trader Joe's announced the next day that masks were no longer mandatory (for "vaccinated" individuals . . .) in the stores. Anecdotal evidence in Florida suggests that the incidence of mask wearing at Wal-Mart fell from 95 to 10 percent in one day; and this is a state where first dose vaccine coverage was only 35 percent at the time.

Besides the fact that the announcement was premature from a public health standpoint, the lack of pre-announcements was also quite odd. For example, it would be clarifying to indicate in advance the criteria to be used to determine when to implement such a decision. As such, it is reasonable to presume that there were reasons other than public health for the CDC to make such an announcement. At the societal unconscious level, or "below" the surface, this once again enacted an undoing of the "pandemic in the mind" while "above" the surface, it probably was to induce non vaccinated individuals to get vaccinated by simulating what the environment could look like the day when it would be all behind. Ultimately, the CDC announcement was, therefore, not a public health statement. It was likely, however, a potentially serious policy mistake; vaccination rates decreased rather than increased at a time when the delta variant was becoming more widespread.

It is important to note that from a psychosocial perspective, statements by President Trump or by some Republican governors that minimized the seriousness of the pandemic and the more recent CDC announcement share similarities. Both are specifically meant to undo the pandemic, either in the form that it is not serious and that nothing will happen or in the form that it has now been overcome. Furthermore, they also both gratify the social system's wishes of eschewing collective efforts at mask wearing, either ex-ante or ex-post. This illustrates that there is far more constancy at the level of psychosocial dynamics than what almost always assumed. Thus, in essence, the social system has likely largely remained unchanged in spite of the transition from a Trump to a Biden presidency. Social systems will only evolve if there has been a psychosocial shock or a period of successful working-through some salient psychosocial issues. Incidentally, minimizing the seriousness of the pandemic was also observed in the UK with Prime Minister Johnson allegedly saying that he wanted "England's chief medical officer to inject him with Covid live on air to prove it was nothing to worry about."[11] The difference though is that Trump sustained his denial even after he caught Covid while Johnson did not; a change of stance on the part of the British Prime Minister that turned out to be, at least until the omicron variant became the dominant strain, beneficial to the UK's management of the pandemic.

Unsurprisingly, in comparison to what could generally be seen in Europe, the measures implemented in the United States were not only less strict but also rarely, if ever, enforced. For example, residential construction and some commerce other than food and medicine were considered essential in the state of Illinois at a time when the city of Chicago had become an epicenter of the pandemic. As a rule, Americans' obsession with individualism; association of personal freedom with absence of infringements; beliefs about limiting the role of the State; and the absence of social safety nets made it difficult to mandate stay at home orders. While the United States is a federation where local officials enjoy far greater latitude in their decision making when compared to their counterparts in, for example, centralized European nations, this does not sufficiently explain the difference in the observed psychosocial dynamics. The costs of the country's response to the Covid-19 pandemic have been so high, the United States quickly becoming the nation with by far the most cases worldwide. From a psychosocial perspective, powerful psychosocial mechanisms, including a majority that were unconscious, must have influenced decisions and collective behaviors. In hindsight, this should not come as a surprise since the extreme polarization in the society, a reflection of the extent to which splitting social defenses are mobilized, can only increase the propensity for public policies to be hijacked as social defenses. While the United States with its technological advances and wealth should have been in a strong position to manage the pandemic well, the country repeatedly squandered opportunities to do so.

What follows illustrates how policy debates in a psychosocially charged environment can quickly get stifled by social defenses. To do so, we now begin by focusing on the reactions to hydroxychloroquine. As is often the case, seemingly unimportant details can often provide rich insights into existing psychosocial dynamics. President Trump's acknowledgment of hydroxychloroquine as a game changer, immediately disavowed and ridiculed by the media and prominent scientists in his administration, is one of those instances. As is well known, the anti-malarial drug hydroxychloroquine was the subject early on of fierce debates about its usefulness in treating Covid-19. This was, for example, the case with the publication of a paper arguing against its use in the prestigious British science journal, The Lancet.[12] The latter's conclusion was, however, immediately criticized (for example in both Spain and the United Kingdom) in light of its reliance on big data; some even suggesting that the data had been manipulated. Regardless, the discussion that follows is not about hydroxychloroquine, a medicine that is no longer judged to be appropriate for the treatment of Covid-19, but rather about the intense psychosocial issues that seemingly surrounded it. Our conclusions are completely independent as to whether or not hydroxychloroquine should even have been recommended or not for the treatment of Covid-19. The swift developments, quick policy reversals, and the intense passions not observed when other potential treatments were discussed strongly suggest that the debate had likely been hijacked by social defenses.

Didier Raoult, the French scientist[13] well-known for his groundbreaking work on emerging infectious diseases, advocated early for a Covid-19 protocol treatment based on the combination of hydroxychloroquine and azithromycin. While never claiming that he had a treatment, he argued that early treatment, ideally at the onset of the infection, decreased significantly the severity and duration of the disease, hence the frequency of complications including the likelihood of death. He also strongly argued against adopting his recommended protocol late in the progression of the virus since the viral load is zero at the latter stages of the disease. This is fundamental. It explains why the medical trials that utilized Professor Raoult's protocol exclusively with seriously ill patients in respiratory distress failed to validate his Covid-19 protocol. On the other hand, when administered to patients early, ideally at the onset of the infection, the results seemed encouraging at the time. As a consequence, the protocol, albeit completely discarded since, ended-up being the first choice of several countries, including several that showed good results at the time in managing the Covid-19 pandemic (e.g., China, South Korea, Thailand, Greece, Portugal, Morocco, and Senegal).

And then on March 21, 2020, @realDonaldTrump tweeted: "HYDROXYCHLOROQUINE & AZITHROMYCIN, taken together, have a real chance to be one of the biggest game changers in the history of medicine." A psychosocial storm quickly erupted.

Data on societal unconscious derivatives is often at its richest at the onset and this was no exception. Thus, the intensity with which splitting social defenses are mobilized in the United States was almost instantly reflected in individuals' reactions to that Covid-19 protocol. Of interest to us here is not whether individuals favored hydroxychloroquine or not but rather the intensity and seeming irrationality with which, regardless of their views, most individuals reacted. Thus, one of the most famous anchormen in the United States laughingly dismissed the protocol as charlatanism on par with injecting bleach, in reference to what President Trump had inquired about during one of his briefings. There is no doubt that President Trump himself has been a significant polarizing figure; to some an object of derision, shame and hate while to others, cult-like adherents of "Make America Great Again," a god-like protecting object shielding them from the abysm. But no matter what the mental representations of the President of the United States might be, to systematically impute to any object associated "in the mind" with the President the psychosocial attributes that are projected onto him is simply enacting the nationwide splitting onto that object. Revealing was the fact that studies dismissing hydroxychloroquine were often reported on US TV as invalidating "Trump's drug" while studies validating it, and there were several abroad, at the time failed to be even mentioned.

Individuals critical of the President for his eschewing of science were, as if they had introjected the behaviors they claimed to despise, behaving in an oddly similar fashion as their object of contempt. While this statement would be vehemently rejected by those opposing the President, to them likely experienced as an attack on identity, it should nevertheless not come as a surprise. After all, supporters and opponents of the polarizing object that Donald Trump represents all share the same social system. At times, social defenses mobilized by one group may not differ greatly from those mobilized by other groups, even when they are split from one another. Most societies would greatly benefit psychosocially from appreciating this.

The paragraph above says nothing about supporting or not supporting Trump. It is, in fact, largely irrelevant when discussing social defenses. All that is argued is that splitting, regardless as to whether or not it was reinforced during a Trump presidency hijacked the debate on hydroxychloroquine, at a time when what was seen as a potential treatment had not yet been rejected by the medical community. The psychosocial mechanism involved is rigorously identical to that of the "hijacking" of a public policy as a social defense. Interestingly, in spite of far greater toxicity and published data on denying its efficacy, the reverse took place with Gilead's Remdesivir. Besides the fact that Remdesivir is far more profitable to Gilead than hydroxychloroquine would have been to Sanofi Pasteur, the social defenses involved are also somewhat different. A Covid-19 treatment discovery by Gilead, an American pharmaceutical company, would not only, like hydroxychloroquine, decrease pandemic anxieties but also potentially provide narcissistic repair to Americans on both sides of the splitting divide. Even Dr. Fauci, the lead member of the White House Coronavirus task force, ridiculed hydroxychloroquine while praising Remdesivir. He, however, startlingly choose to do so the same day that a study doubting the efficacy of the latter had come out and even acknowledged that impact on mortality had not even been part of the study.

As is well known, while largely unconscious, social defenses become an intrinsic part of a social system. As such, members of the society often introject them. This was, in our view, the case with Dr. Fauci's behavior in this specific case. This was further exacerbated when President Trump revealed that he was taking hydroxychloroquine preventively. While the president no doubt enjoyed being purposely divisive and courting controversies, the reactions condemning President Trump reached a paroxysm that revealed the intensity with which hydroxychloroquine embodied the intense splitting that had taken the entire nation hostage. Social media postings critical of the president were urging him to continue his treatment under the belief that he would soon succumb while Nancy Pelosi, the speaker of the House of Representatives, slammed the president for taking the medication and denigrated him by saying that hydroxychloroquine could be harmful since he was morbidly obese. The bickering in Washington escalated on something that should never have become the main topic of the media. After all, there was still at the time a large-scale clinical trial in France whereas doctors and nurses exposed to Covid-19 through their patients were taking the same treatment preventively. In fact, Morocco, a country that has continuously managed the pandemic well, attributed its early success in fighting the pandemic to its protocol of administering the drug combination as close as possible to the onset of the infection.

The psychosocial dynamics discussed above were sadly also observed with the socially charged debates and enactments on lockdowns, whether or not to put them in place and under what conditions; on the distribution of responsibilities between the federal government and individual states; as well as on masks as already mentioned in the previous section. The inability to discuss public policies concerning the issues above on their merits alone, the debate themselves hijacked by social defenses, rarely bodes well. With mental representations of the pandemic and public policy responses influenced by social defenses, decisions were often reversed (e.g., Georgia was one of the last states to impose a lockdown but reversed it soon after) and enactments defiant, if not violent. The latter was, for example, the case with the multitude of disruptive "Corona parties" that took place in Chicago and, as mentioned earlier, extreme-right armed demonstrators protesting the lockdowns right outside the Michigan's Governor office. The measures adopted in the United States were often vague and poorly enforced because the authorities ended up acting upon societal ambivalence; something that was likely "communicated" to them in response to the numerous unconscious collusions that exist within a social system. As a consequence, most states failed at adopting and implementing a consistent policy framework.

We now turn to what may have been the most salient psychosocial dynamics that defined the United States' encounter with the pandemic. These include:

i. Splitting, which led to aggression and manic-depressive attitudes toward the pandemic;
ii. Narcissism that hampered the ability to rally collectively and in solidarity with one another to manage the pandemic; and

iii. Indifference and meaninglessness, which is key to explaining the psychosocial failure of the United States to confront the pandemic successfully.

The analysis that follows concludes that it is together-yet-alone that Americans faced the pandemic.

As mentioned earlier, the intensity with which the "War of the Masks" played out truly stands out. Almost instantly, masks became objects on which the already existing societal splitting became displayed. While empathic availability and internalized feelings of sharing a space and a destiny turned out, at last initially, to be conducive for the populations of several countries to show solidarity and the willingness to do something on behalf of the common good, this was not the case in the United States. For example, the Governor of North Dakota had to plead with his constituents to tolerate those wishing to wear masks and to not resort to violence. In light of the intensity of the feelings surrounding masks and the potential risks of violent reactions (i.e., psychosocial enactments), the Governor quickly understood that he needed to adopt a very mild tone to avoid fueling violence; a strong indication in our view of the highly regressed psychosocial dynamics at play in the United States. There were several incidents of individuals being aggressively pressured to take off their masks; a sign that to some the mask had become an attack on the group's identity. Furthermore, there were also violent reprisals by those that were requested to wear a mask in areas where they had been made compulsory in order to protect the community. Refusing the injunction to abide by the rules, offenders were often seen spitting onto the face of those that had made the request. By mimicking transmitting the virus, the deliberate retaliatory gesture was not only a grotesque and revolting display of aggression but also a symbolic murder. The United States increasingly felt like a place that had sunk to a new low at a time when solidarity and coming together should have prevailed.

The manic depressive-like attitudes towards the pandemic as a consequence of the splitting suggest that the country was ill prepared to work through the psychosocial dynamics that arose. What ensued turned out to be a self-inflicted injury that turned out to be quite costly. The country, several states unable to successfully implement lockdowns, experienced a much larger number of cases and deaths than should otherwise have been the case. While splitting made it impossible to attain an adequate nationwide consensus on public policy responses, other psychosocial mechanisms were also involved.

Extreme individualism, a consequence of a transaction-based society promoting well being at the individual rather than the collective level, is destroying the social compact.[14] From a psychosocial perspective, the implication is that members of society are losing the capacity to identify with one another, particularly with those that belong to different groups. This promotes a culture of narcissism. See, Lasch (1979). As a consequence, the framing of public health messages, particularly with respect to the use of protective masks as public acts of solidarity and members of society protecting one another rather than only themselves, could not possibly have been well received. As with any public policy, the messaging should have taken into account the existing psychosocial dynamics; emphasizing in this case personal as well as group wellbeing. Sadly, the United States stands out as one of the few nations where feelings and acts of togetherness in facing the pandemic were too few and far between. While the situation evolved for the better once the administration of President Biden began to implement the national vaccine efforts, the social defenses mobilized remained the same. We return to this topic in chapter 3.

Almost all countries, even those that experienced slippages in their ability to maintain the required collective discipline to overcome the pandemic, showed the mettle to go through the collective effort required to successfully address the pandemic. This was almost never the case in the United States. But societies cannot afford too many "free-riders" in a pandemic caused by a respiratory pathogen. This creates a negative externality whereas the deliberate refusal to comply by some implies that the entire group becomes negatively impacted, not only because extending restrictive measures hurts the economy but also because it can promote the emergence of new variants that can be more contagious, more lethal or resistant to existing vaccines. Unlike during the times of the Greatest Generation,[15] there exists little willingness and capacity today for the kind of collective sacrifices that were the hallmarks of earlier times.

This eclipse of the collective is also due to the perverse impact of the communication technology revolution, which has paradoxically brought individuals closer together while at the same time isolating them from one another. See, Turkle (2011). This is key to understanding the growing interpersonal indifference that is becoming so pervasive in modern societies, particularly the United States. In making social interactions transactional, through rewards by comments, likes and number of followers, social media are destroying genuine communication. Social media is a psychosocial experiment on a worldwide scale whose seductiveness is taking us into unchartered waters. Yet, one thing that is already clear is its propensity to destroy critical thinking. Furthermore, while sensationalized news media makes us aware of suffering anywhere in the world, it also desensitizes us; a modern-day banality of evil also encouraged by the commercialization of the internet purposely promoting a reduced attention span. Lastly, the convenience of modern day living for some, where almost anything can be purchased with an effortless click on a computer and often delivered to one's home, has made daily interactions nearly disappear.

The latter point takes us to the heart of the perverse nature that technology can have on psychosocial dynamics. In a powerful article published in The Guardian, a British journalist argues that while "libidinal" is probably the last word that comes to mind when we think of transactions performed on the likes of Amazon on the internet, it is, in fact, a particularly relevant concept.[16] Technologies today makes it possible for many to instantly and effortlessly satisfy almost any desire with a simple click of a button from a home computer. Transactions today can be therefore thought as being deliberately structured to satisfy libidinal urges for instant gratification in order to promote unabashed consumerism. Although many consumers understand that this destroy society's aliveness by eliminating contacts with shopkeepers and others, the libidinal urge is manipulated, including by the advertisement industry, in such a way that it becomes next to impossible to resist.

The consequence has been an epidemic of indifference to one another, which has been unusually resilient precisely because of the libidinal underpinnings identified above. It is, therefore, together yet alone that Americans faced the pandemic. The willingness to sacrifice anything on behalf of the group could not be mustered; protective gestures, if undertaken, were only adopted on one's own behalf rather than on the group's behalf. Unsurprisingly, this became a nearly insurmountable obstacle during a pandemic whose successful management required solidarity and coordination of protective measures amongst the population. To make things worse, psychosocial changes induced by markets are rarely resisted because the incentive structure is precisely designed to have those changes experienced as chosen preferences.

In the relentless submission to the behaviors imposed by the markets and the media, shared meaning other than individualism is ultimately lost. As argued by Boccara (2014), a society's emotional wellbeing collapses at its deepest level once that kind of meaning is lost. As a rule, a loss of meaning is a strong indicator that a society will find itself unable to cope with whatever changes (e.g., economic, technological, political, etc) it is facing. This was in evidence in the way the United States chose to approach the pandemic. The disappearing sense of relatedness meant that the pandemic could only be faced from the individual's perspective; a psychosocial aspect which significantly undermined compliance with mask wearing and lockdowns. There were no "others in the mind" to act in solidarity with. Meaninglessness had, at least in that instance, killed the ability and the will to sacrifice anything on behalf of the society.

Finally, as if all the stumbling blocks identified earlier were not enough, managing the pandemic was further hampered by narcissistic denial; a social defense mobilized in this case to shield the group from unbearable shame. While triumphalism and blind faith in American exceptionalism have continuously made the country romance[17] of being the "most powerful and preferred nation" particularly resilient, the pandemic challenged this. Quickly becoming one of the worst countries managing the pandemic, as seen in both number of cases and, to a lesser extent, in death per capita, likely resulted in a collective narcissistic injury that had to be defended against. And yet, the social system almost always acted as if it did not know. Strikingly, there was almost no mention, nothing imprinted in the national conscience, of the extreme number of deaths that has outpaced India's in spite of the latter's delta wave. It exceeded 750,000 by mid-October 2021. Indifference reigned supreme.

As already seen earlier, splitting, which is what the extreme polarization represents, was one of the main social defenses mobilized. As such, mental representations and potential policy responses to the management of Covid-19 were all "hijacked" by the splitting that permeates the entire social system. Since splitting is a defense against persecutory "bad" objects, it is often accompanied by denial of the associated fear, which in turn leads to the mobilization, as a social defense, of feelings of invincibility. The refusal to acknowledge the seriousness of the pandemic became a way to annihilate the persecutory "bad" object.

The wish to maintain a past glory, whose loss was being made even starker by the pandemic, led to collusive denial. However, enacting rebirth fantasies, through denial-induced premature re-opening of states during Covid-19, turned out to be quite costly in psychosocial terms; the social system losing its capacity to work through even further. The latter point is fundamental since ultimately whether or not psychosocial issues become overwhelming depends upon that social system's capacity to work though the underlying issues; in other words, its capacity to internalize and question its own psychosocial dynamics. For example, the fixation with maintaining at all cost grandiose and omnipotence fantasies, in evidence with both the "Make America Great Again" and the "America is back" mantras, likely implies the mobilization of often-regressed social defenses that can be damaging to the country. Thus, mobilizing social defenses to restore omnipotence, what exceptionalism and the associated feelings of superiority is all about, was unlikely to work with an exogenous event for which there was little, if anything, that the nation could do at first. The latter is what made the pandemic such a formidable psychosocial challenge to the United States as a social system. Furthermore, while splitting allowed defensive deflection of the responsibility onto the "Other," meaning onto groups split from one's group of affiliation, it became increasingly hard to reconcile the early catastrophic mismanagement of Covid-19 with the massive idealization of the country that permeates the society.

In response, the massive, and, at least initially, successful, vaccine drive that started under the Biden administration turned out to also be experienced as the perfect social defense to undo the unbearable shame and nearly insurmountable anxieties that had the capacity to quickly overwhelm the nation. In preventing a forceful de-idealization of the country, the vaccine drives also acted as a psychosocial policy: defensively, it performed a repair act. Unfortunately, that was its potential downfall as vaccines were simultaneously endowed with magical qualities but also loathed. We return to this topic in the next chapter.

Unlike Europe, there was relatively less splitting across vaccination status in the United States. The main reason behind this is that the United States chose not to resort to the kind of Covid health passes that became so prevalent in Europe. The adoption of such pass would have significantly conflicted with the individualism and, as a consequence, with the greater acknowledgment of differences that is one of the hallmarks of the United States as a social system. The adoption of Covid health passes elsewhere promoted mental representations of unvaccinated individuals as pariahs that had to be excluded from shared spaces (e.g., restaurants, some forms of public transportation, entertainment venues). Even when it became common knowledge that vaccinated individuals could still harbor and transmit the virus; unvaccinated individuals remained the sole repository of society's internal aggression in response to the anxieties created by the pandemic; something plainly in evidence with Austria's decision in November 2021 to re-confine unvaccinated individuals. And yet at the same time, Belgium de facto recognized the inadequacy of relying on Covid passes allowing freedom of movement to vaccinated individuals since it also added a testing requirement (in addition to the vaccines) for some activities. Idealization of vaccines, a topic discussed in the next chapter that focuses on the social defenses once vaccines became available, encouraged the mobilization of splitting social defenses.

NOTES

1. Joint WHO-China study, "WHO-convened global study of SARS-CoV-2 origins: China Part," *World Health Organization Publications*, March 30, 2021.
2. "Investigate the origins of COVID-19," *Science*, Vol. 372, Issue 3543, May 14, 2021, https://science.sciencemag.org/content/372/6543/694.1.full.
3. "Covid-19: enquête sur le mystère des origines d'une pandémie mondiale," *France 2*, https://www.francetvinfo.fr/sante/maladie/coronavirus/video-coronavirus-le-mystere-des-origines_4328629.html, March 11, 2021.
4. "Opinion: State Department cables warned of safety issues at Wuhan lab studying bat coronaviruses," *Washington Post*, https://www.washingtonpost.com/opinions/2020/04/14/state-department-cables-warned-safety-issues-wuhan-lab-studying-bat-coronaviruses/, April 14, 2020.

5. These include Belarus, Burundi, Iceland, Nicaragua, South Korea, Sweden, and Uruguay. Japan and Taiwan resorted to local lockdowns in 2021.

6. We are limiting to the psychosocial issues here. It is nevertheless important to note that politicians also benefitted from the lockdowns as they provided opportunities to stifle social protests (e.g., Colombia).

7. The latter often resulting on more pressure on the environment, as is the case in the Amazon rainforest in Brazil.

8. R0 must fall before 1, the ideal—and prerequisite—condition to end lockdowns, for an epidemic to disappear.

9. See, for example, "How Masks Went From Don't-Wear to Must-Have," *Wired,* https://www.wired.com/story/how-masks-went-from-dont-wear-to-must-have/, July 2, 2020; "How did facemasks become a political issue in America?," *The Guardian,* https://www.theguardian.com/world/2020/jun/29/face-masks-us-politics-coronavirus, June 29, 2020; and "COVID-19 mask mandates in Wisconsin and elsewhere spark 'my body, my choice' hypocrisy," *NBC News*, https://www.nbcnews.com/think/opinion/covid-19-mask-mandates-wisconsin-elsewhere-spark-my-body-my-ncna1235535, August 3, 2020.

10. In October 2020, conspirators, unhappy with the Governor's Covid restrictions, planned to storm the Capitol, take hostages, and kill the Governor.

11. As reported by Dominic Cummings, the man who served Boris Johnson as his most senior adviser on Covid-19. See, https://www.cnn.com/2021/05/26/uk/dominic-cummings-boris-johnson-pandemic-handling-intl-gbr/index.html, May 26, 2021.

12. Incidentally, there were several criticisms, even from within the Lancet, of the author's approach; an odd development for an article accepted for publication by such a prestigious journal. The article had to be retracted later. See, https://www.thelancet.com/journals/lancet/article/PIIS0140-6736(20)31180-6/fulltext, May 22, 2020.

13. Professor Raoult who holds numerous prestigious awards and honors is the most cited microbiologist in Europe and the most published in France. He and his team in Marseille have identified 380 new bacterial species and 63 viruses, and sequenced 290 bacterial genomes. His stance during the pandemic was nevertheless heavily criticized in France.

14.The "concept of "rugged individualism" is central to the United States' mythos. This, in turn, has led to difficult to manage tensions between each person's individual rights and collective responsibilities. While the balance between the two that is considered appropriate by the two main political parties differ, our interest lies in the psychosocial aspects of this, which we believe has more to do with economics and technology than political orientation.

15. The well-known American journalist, Tom Brokaw, coined the term. It designates the generation that lived through both the Great Depression and World War II and displayed an extraordinary sense of collective solidarity and sacrifice.

16. "We know Amazon is killing the high street, so why do we keep clicking on 'buy now'?," *The Guardian*, https://www.theguardian.com/commentisfree/2021/apr/26/amazon-killing-the-high-street-online-shopping, April 26, 2021.

17. The country romance is defined by the idealized mental representations that need to be sustained in order to maintain a set of narratives that define the collective identity.

Chapter 3

Vaccines and their Vicissitudes

This chapter continues with identifying the social defenses mobilized during the pandemic by shifting the focus on the psychosocial dynamics that arose once vaccines were made available. In enabling a defensively wished for magical undoing of the pandemic, vaccines also led a majority of nations to adopt a risky "live with the virus" position, which in turn led to a near complete abandonment of protective gestures.

TODAY IS A GREAT DAY FOR SCIENCE AND FOR HUMANITY: MAGICAL UNDOING

A great day for humanity is how Albert Bourla, the chairman and CEO of Pfizer announced the Phase 3 trial results of the Covid vaccine based on messenger RNA technology developed by Biotech. The news that a vaccine with 90 percent effectiveness, updated to 95 percent a week later, had been found sent stocks rallying everywhere, hope spreading worldwide that the pandemic could soon be over, thanks to the miracle news that had just been announced.

The world immediately reacted "as if" the pandemic could be undone; magically transforming in the process its wish for an undoing into a reality. This is absolutely key to understanding the psychosocial dynamics underpinning the pandemic and how they, in turn, influenced the outcome. Once an object experienced as having the capacity to miraculously undo pandemic anxieties became available, the capacity for thinking, as if psychosocial constraints were no longer relevant, quickly evaporated. As such, there was little questioning of the potential consequences of using—for the first time ever- messenger RNA technology. Yet one cannot exclude, even if the biotech companies have argued the opposite, that the information embedded in the vaccine might eventually be integrated into the DNA of current and hence future generations. While the Nobel Prize winner Luc Montagnier brought up the idea first,[1] others also discussed it with, for example, the fact that the herpes virus as well as that of a Brazilian parasite insert their code into the DNA and can be transmitted from mother to child.[2] Vaccines-linked increased risks of cancers were also brought up by some researchers. With this topic falling outside the book's area of expertise, the purpose here is not to express a theoretical opinion but rather that collective (and individual) thinking may be blurred by the nature of the social defenses mobilized. Thus, on a topic of vital importance, collective thinking was once again impacted by the social defenses. This would be particularly relevant at a time of high anxieties as could only have been the case when vaccines first became available almost a year after the pandemic began. Our collective awareness of this would, by nature, remain absent since the process of mobilizing social defenses is largely unconscious. It is precisely because unconscious processes "purposely" remain hidden that it becomes paramount to raise their awareness and elucidate how they function and influence outcomes.

Magical thinking subverts genuine critical thinking since it replaces reality by what is defensively wished for. This was, for example, reflected in the legion of statements arguing against mask wearing outside. While it is correct that risks of outdoor transmission of Covid-19 are technically very low, it does not necessarily imply, as was discussed in the previous chapter, that policies eliminating mask mandates were always justified. Enactments in response to magical wishes to undo the pandemic are likely to induce behaviors that are not compatible with the goals of the policies. For example, from a psychosocial perspective, respecting social distancing is an irruption of reality (a reminder that Covid-19 is still there), which hampers the group's capacity to maintain "in the mind" the desperately wished for and needed undoing. Compliance, once these social defenses are mobilized, can only falter. While some in the scientific community argued that there had not been a single beach cluster, this was not the case; both the Miami winter party festival and Spring break lead to several cases and deaths. After all, the largest single most spreading event in the world, the once in twelve years Kumbh Mela in India, which attracted 9.1 million pilgrims in a scaled down version from January 14 to April 27, 2021, took place outside. Incidentally, the same was also observed in Vietnam; a country essentially without Covid-19 virus circulation until June 2021 but that nevertheless witnessed a sharply accelerating rate of infection as a consequence of large gatherings outside.[3]

Similarly, the French Prime Minister, as well as the medical community, was horrified at the behaviors, even if predictable, shunning all protective gestures observed in France the day its terraces reopened on May 19, 2021. But, on that very same day, there was a well publicized visit to a terrace by President Macron accompanied by his Prime Minister to celebrate that France's cherished way of life was back. Yet in doing so, they linked the pandemic to the disappearance of a way of life, a loss of identity that would—especially in France today—be anxiety provoking. They, therefore, choreographed a public repair act in the form of an undoing that could only encourage the excessive behaviors observed that day. In fact, several members of the government did the same; French news showing the finance minister sipping a cup of coffee in a terrace in Paris. And yet, Paris had an incidence rate the day before of 181 per 100,000, while the threshold considered safe for reopening had been fixed at 50 by the French authorities.

As a rule, message consistency regarding compliance with protective gestures until those can be deemed no longer essential is crucial for policy announcements to also be able to incorporate into their timing the nature of the existing social defenses. In that respect pre-announced criteria rather than ad-hoc announcements could be quite useful. The situation in France or the United States contrasts with that of Singapore; a country that had replaced New Zealand in July 2021 at the top position in Bloomberg's Covid Resilience Ranking. The key to Singapore' success, as was also the case with New Zealand, is that small outbreaks were systematically quickly suppressed with strict measures (e.g., contact tracing and isolation). As a consequence, life has been near normal with the exception of the first and only lockdown at the onset of the pandemic. This, however, came at a cost as migrant workers ended-up being strictly monitored in the island nation. Nevertheless, the extraordinary success of Singapore, notwithstanding the fact that the nation's governance structure made it easier to impose restrictions on the population, highlights the importance of policy responses that are, thanks to their consistency and rule-basis, less likely to be influenced by psychosocial dynamics. Incidentally, in spite of a very low virus circulation, Singapore has to this day maintained a strict mask mandate, including outdoors. It also quickly responded to a small rise in cases in May 2021 by tightening security at the airport, which had experienced a cluster of cases. Incorporating psychosocial analysis in policy formulation and timing also decreases the probability of having to reverse policies, as was the case with France going in and out of lockdowns.

The reason that magical thinking was mobilized in response to the collective wish to undo the pandemic is first and foremost that the level of anxiety was extremely high. It had, after all, led the entire planet to come to a standstill; an eerie situation to witness that from the very start led vaccines to be massively idealized. With hindsight, had more countries faced the pandemic along the lines of what was observed in South Korea, Singapore, or New Zealand, magical thinking would not necessarily have been mobilized to the extent that it was in so many countries worldwide. Far from an elusive outcome, managing like the four countries mentioned above could also have been a reachable goal for most other nations. It would have required incorporating psychosocial and systems dynamics thinking into public policies to prevent the mobilization of social defenses that hampered the management of the pandemic. However, managing the psychosocial environment needs to be sustained because complacency or fatigue can derail the efforts. An example of this is turning a blind eye to loopholes in what are otherwise well designed and enforced surveillance policies. This is, sadly, the story of Taiwan, which did not report a single infection from April to December 2020 but subsequently faced a surge in infection while less than one percent of its population had been vaccinated.

Magical thinking often leads to odd outcomes. For example, it seems to have benefitted Pfizer the most since it became massive idealized following the pharmaceutical company becoming the first to publish its phase 3 results and the first to obtain approval for emergency use in any country (in the UK on December 2). At least in the United States, there is some evidence that mental representations of the so-called "Pfizer vaccine" were such that receiving it was experienced as belonging to a coveted special club; an "accomplishment" that many felt prone to share on social media accounts. As such, an article in the Atlantic describes how on "Pfizer elitism seems to have originated on TikTok, where the vaccine hierarchy has been most concretely outlined," suggesting that it came out of American culture.[4] We would rephrase instead that it originates with magical thinking; hence the way the US has functioned as a social system during the pandemic. To be fair, the reliability data on the so-called "Pfizer vaccine," including on the way it protects from variants was, at least until end-June 2021, quite good. Regardless, the idealization began prior to that data being available, which in turn was seen as validating the early idealization. Yet, psychosocial dynamics can evolve things quickly. Towards the end of the Summer 2021, as the delta variant became dominant nearly everywhere, it became increasingly clear that breakthrough infections occurred with far greater frequency than what the public had been led to believe. While the risks of hospitalization and deaths remained relatively low, the protection offered by the mRNA vaccines, particularly Pfizer was much lower than what the massive idealization buttressed by the 95 percent effectiveness figure given at the onset had led everyone to expect. At the same time, several countries began advocating for a third injection. The rapidity at which the recommendations are changing is prone to destroying trust and slowing down vaccination rates. Once again, the overall level of anxieties is too high for governments not to work on public health policy and dialogue from a psychosocial and system dynamics perspective. The same story holds with omicron, a variant whose apparition quickly eroded the low level of trust that already existed.

Unfortunately, the massive idealization of the vaccines appears to have also contributed to feelings of entitlement. In fact, the vaccination campaigns often stressed that aspect in emphasizing what vaccinated individuals could do in contrast to what, in theory at least, unvaccinated individuals could not. Vaccines became, at the expense of all other protective measures, the ticket to be "liberated." This, in turn, exacerbated the lack of solidarity that, except at the very beginning, had already become a dominant feature of many nations facing the pandemic. Legislation excluding unvaccinated individuals from most activities quickly followed. Thus, the way the story unfolded turned out not to be what the WHO had hoped for; sublime moments of "we are all in this together" quickly dissipating into individuals retreating into the safety of looking for themselves and no one else. And, what turned out to be true within most societies also held for the ways in which most nations engaged with one another. The chimera of the entire world coming together in the search for a vaccine quickly evaporated once vaccines became available. With vaccines as magical objects of desire, hoarding replaced sharing. In spite of facing a truly shared crisis for the very first time, the world as a whole acted overall as a collection of social systems separated from one another by rigid boundaries.

To this, we now turn by focusing on the related topics of waiving patent rights, boosting production, and vaccine sharing.

Today's pharmaceutical companies have become providers of branding, testing, and manufacturing to smaller biotech companies that are the ones undertaking the research. In doing so, they hugely benefit, albeit indirectly, from the significant financial assistance afforded to those companies by the public sector and private foundations. The US government alone spent billions of dollars funding vaccine research. And yet, while Moderna committed to waiving enforcement of its patents, Pfizer did not. This would have been unthinkable when smallpox was eradicated or when penicillin was produced during World War II. Unfortunately, the severity of the pandemic and the need to attempt to vaccinate as many people worldwide as possible—regardless of borders—appeared as secondary to potential future profits. What could not be eradicated once and for all seems now bound to become a much longer struggle; the virus always finding paths to replicate and mutate. While the pharmaceutical companies undoubtedly understood the risk, it seems nevertheless that they might have perversely colluded to adopt a vaccine distribution model had has a greater propensity for making the disease endemic, hence increasing overall profits. Furthermore, without much scientific evidence at the time, and before the likelihood of breakthrough infections was known to be higher than originally expected, Pfizer was already suggesting the need for a third booster shot. The sequential distribution of vaccines geographically is sadly something that the social systems in the countries that benefitted from vaccines first were unable to overcome; be it through legislation or the mobilization of social defenses. In fact, in the midst of India seeing an exponential rise in infections, Bill Gates nevertheless indicated that companies not releasing patents abroad was not necessarily the main constraint[5] while other leading public figures such as Nobel laureate Joe Stiglitz condemned this as morally wrong and foolish.[6] A genuine understanding of the underlying dynamics, as a prerequisite to changing them, requires analyzing the social system as a whole from both an "above" the surface and a "below" the surface perspective. Splitting between the have's and have not's, something ingrained in social systems worldwide, can become extraordinarily resilient.

It is actually not clear that lifting patents would make a difference. While patent rights are considered intellectual property, the latter comprises copyrights, patents, trademarks, and trade secrets. Not enforcing patents does not appear to be the real constraint at this time since all that matters is enabling countries to produce vaccines as fast as possible. Doing so seems to require instead focusing on export restrictions on vaccine components, making the vaccines affordable (which companies are doing by segmenting their prices according to a country's level of income), and ramping up production. These are essentially what the EU proposed to the World Trade Organizations (WTO). Furthermore, WTO rules allow countries to grant licenses to manufacturers without the consent of the patent holder if the vaccines are provided at cost.

The issue above is highly technical from a legal standpoint and is, as such, outside our areas of interest. What is at stake from a psychosocial point of view is what the WHO director has appropriately named "vaccine apartheid," a point actually raised months earlier by the executive director of the Joint United Nations Program on HIV/AIDS (UNAIDS) in response to South Africa paying more than double what the EU was charged for the Astra Zeneca vaccine.

FROM VACCINE APARTHEID TO THE EMERGENCE OF SIGNIFICANT PSYCHOSOCIAL FAULT LINES

The entitlement and greed that has permeated Western societies was played out on the world stage and, as a consequence, left the "have not's" behind while the "have's" selfishly hoarded vaccines to ensure that their own population would be protected first. Thus, until it felt pressured to reverse that decision, the United States for several months kept a stockpile of Astra Zeneca vaccines that it knew it would never use. Along similar lines, Israel, the most vaccinated country in the world at the time (May 2021), decided not to provide vaccines to West Bank Palestinians (save those individuals who commuted daily to work in Israel). It is hard to believe that the Israeli health authorities would deliberately take such a risky decision in light of the two populations sharing the same epidemiological space. While "rationally," the discussions centered on whether it was Israel or the Palestinian Authority that had jurisdiction on a vaccination campaign, the psychosocial fact remains that Israel's intense splitting from its Palestinian neighbors meant that social defenses were also likely "hijacking" a policy whose choice, not only on humanitarian but also on public health grounds, should have been a foregone conclusion. But in a highly risky move from an epidemiological standpoint, Israel—while it was exporting surplus doses to India—"chose" to ignore its neighbors in the West Bank.

Thus, the individualism decried earlier in the United States also manifested itself at the level of entire social systems elsewhere leading to a large share of the developing world being deprived of vaccines. Magical thinking contributed to reinforcing national exclusionary sentiments, which in turn led to a highly unequal access to vaccines across nations. This is counterintuitive since the pandemic will not be over until it is over globally. But, while the virus itself knows no boundaries, the mobilization of social defenses across individual nations does. This led the WHO to ask wealthy nations to donate vaccine doses to poorer nations instead of starting to vaccinate children. With a large share of the developing world still not capable of vaccinating their most vulnerable and their health care workers, the WHO indicated that the moral catastrophe that they had warned about in January 2021 (when vaccinations started) was now unfolding. Heading the recommendations issued by WHO made sense at the time since several western countries had then not yet entered a new phase of the pandemic. The risk of unvaccinated individuals becoming infected was thought to be much lower in countries where a large share of the adult population was fully vaccinated. Unfortunately, this was all upended with the increased contagiousness of the delta variant, which quickly became the dominating variant. Under pressure from the EU, Pfizer, Moderna, and Johnson & Johnson agreed to supply billions of doses at cost to low-income countries. While laudable, the vaccines were scheduled to only reach the poorer countries by the end of 2021 or early 2022, which could only increase the duration and severity of the pandemic. The story repeated itself in the fall of 2021 as Western nations began focusing on their booster campaigns while continuing to ignore pleas for vaccines from nations that were still struggling to get their vaccination campaigns under way. It does not make sense to rely on vaccines alone during an airborne pandemic unless vaccination can be simultaneous nearly everywhere, which is essentially an impossible task.

In the case of Sub-Saharan Africa, the region at the greatest disadvantage regarding vaccine availability, most of the vaccines available are sourced through Covax, the UN initiative whose goal is to promote an equitable access to vaccines for all countries. But towards the end of Fall 2021, the majority of the countries covered by the scheme still struggled to find vaccines and often had to settle on vaccines considered less adapted to their epidemiological situation (e.g., Astra Zeneca for the South African variant). The situation in Sub-Saharan Africa was further exacerbated when nations found themselves unable of administering second doses once India stopped exporting vaccines due to the catastrophic turn that the pandemic had taken there. Psychosocially, the then increasing distrust worldwide in Astra Zeneca due to thromboses coupled with both the anxiety and the humiliation-induced shame among African nations of being the recipients of technology or products shunned by more developed nations, led to many unused doses being discarded in spite of vaccine shortages. This was, for example, the case in South Sudan and in the Democratic Republic of Congo. In Malawi, the health authorities felt that they had no choice but to incinerate publicly expired doses to avoid further eroding the public trust. The government rightly understood that, as a consequence of the anxiety and shame mentioned earlier, the population in Malawi would lose all trust in the vaccines. This was not a risk they were willing to take. And a disappearance of trust is also something with which the authorities in Cote d'Ivoire were confronted.

This West African nation has been beset by a wave of social media driven disinformation about the vaccine, which was also reinforced by a French TV program in which French doctors' comments were misinterpreted as suggesting that potential vaccines should be experimented first in Africa. Needless to say, this takes us immediately back to the anxiety and shame mentioned earlier surrounding the notion of African populations being used by the West. For one nation, Tanzania, this anxiety and shame contributed to one of the most acute denials observed. On May 15, 2020, the then president John Magafulli announced that the pandemic had completely ended. In an effort to validate this delusional undoing, the country stopped reporting any pandemic related data. The country ended up not reporting a single new case until more than a year later and then only reported weekly one or two cases a day, which was undeniably too low. Furthermore, not a single dose of vaccine—there could not possibly be any need for them—was ordered! Sadly, but ironically, President Magafulli died of Covid-19, albeit reported as heart complications, a year later on May 17, 2021. Fortunately, the President's successor adopted public health policies more consistent with the reality, although data had still not been reported by the end of June 2021.

As one could expect, mistrust and resistance to vaccines has not been limited to Sub-Saharan Africa. The anxieties brought up by the pandemic were also responded to with a significant denial of what was unfolding. A denial social defense, a wish not to know, shares an important similarity with the magical thinking underpinning an undoing social defense. In both cases, the perceived seriousness of the pandemic is weakened since the threat is either diminished (what denial accomplishes) or thought to be capable of being magically resolved (what magical thinking accomplishes). As such, public concern about Covid-19 vaccines was higher amongst those who downplayed the seriousness of the pandemic.

It is also quite telling that vaccination rates in the United States considerably slowed down in the summer of 2021, right at the time when it was becoming clear that the increasing presence of the delta variant was becoming a threat. The country was, as a consequence, totally overwhelmed by the pandemic. Without in-depth psychosocial assessments, it is not possible to genuinely understand the psychosocial dynamics involved. While purely hypothetical, one cannot exclude the mobilization of retaliatory social defenses whose purpose would be to sabotage the public health policies implemented to fight Covid-19 as a way to validate, in a "I told you so" fashion, mental representations of the pandemic as an orchestrated plot by the elites. After all, this would probably be the psychosocial interpretation of the "Stop the Steal" movement, whose attacks on democracy in the United States are part of an undoing through a denial (of Trump's loss to Biden) social defense. The social defenses mobilized in support of the "Stop the Steal" movement, are identical to those mobilized in support of the "Stop the Vaccines" movement. In both cases, the social defenses mobilized are, in the mind of those that are mobilizing them, retaliatory attacks on the elites. And following the 2021 United Nations Climate Change conference (COP26), the anti-vaccines movement also started shifting its focus to denying the appropriateness of the advocated measures to fight climate change. While the above is likely to have held at the time, confidence in the vaccines eroded further once it was established, contrary to what the general public had been led to believe, that the immunity offered by the vaccines declined quite fast. And this, in spite of vaccines shown to be very good at protecting from serious complications. In line with the magical thinking that surrounded the vaccines, a narrative of a uniquely powerful vaccine was adopted. Unfortunately, waning immunity made maintaining magical thinking nearly impossible. The psychosocial equilibrium that had allowed, in large part through a deliberate abandonment of the protective gestures, a magical undoing of the pandemic had been broken. Rather than return to a systematic and disciplined adoption of protective measures, Covid-19 public health policies became increasingly resisted. The bitter disappointment that followed, the trust in governments and the big pharmaceutical having eroded quickly, led to the worsening outcomes that Europe and the United States experienced starting mid-November 2021; a situation that exploded with the arrival of the omicron variant.

Public policy should never be implemented without a deep understanding of the underlying psychosocial issues. Once anxieties ceased to be contained by the magical thinking that had been mobilized, it became paramount to mobilize alternative social defenses. Denial of the unique challenges and risks of having Covid-19 becoming endemic quickly followed. Shunning mask wearing led to the mobilization of increasingly regressive social defenses; splitting across vaccination status rather than potentially more inclusive approaches focused on protective measures.

However, successful eradication of Covid-19 would have required the (nearly simultaneous) vaccination of a large segment of the population. Until then, reliance on protective gestures should not have been abandoned. As already argued, the risk of mass vaccination campaigns faltering was due to the disease becoming endemic; the production of antibodies among a vaccinated population highly exposed to a still circulating virus likely leading to the emergence of new strains, including more virulent and contagious ones that would be resistant to those antibodies. To succeed in increasing coverage, vaccination campaigns will need to genuinely understand, at both the conscious and unconscious levels, the sources of resistance for different groups in each society. As referred to earlier, resistance could, for example, be due to experiencing vaccines as attacks on identity; to perceiving them as "bad" objects contaminated from a state in which one has no trust in, or to genuine medical concerns.

A common thread throughout the book so far has been that regardless of how various nations were able to manage the pandemic, the underlying psychosocial dynamics were nothing less than daunting. Looking into the future, the psychosocial fault lines that have already emerged and that are expected could even be worse.

On the economic front, or "above" the surface, these have been reflected in drastically changing behaviors. These include:

1. Labor market with changing preferences towards employment (e.g., less willingness to return to certain jobs, increased acceptance of virtual offices);
2. Fiscal policy with governments' increased tolerance of public debt;
3. Monetary policy with central banks' increased tolerance of inflation; and
4. Consumption, notably in real estate where demand and supply changed so quickly that housing prices exploded; the entire world going on a housing spree.

On the job market, the labor force participation rate has yet to recover. While the reluctance to go back to one's job can be partially explained by the presence of fiscal incentives (e.g., income support payments from the State) and, more importantly health concerns (e.g., working with customers not wearing masks) as well as the low availability of child care, it seems that the anxieties brought up by the pandemic, whether they were verbalized or not, have led individuals to a standstill. The high number of long-term unemployed suggests a demand-constrained job market while the number of firms struggling to find workers suggests a supply-constrained one. As economies seemed poised to recover, individuals appeared to need time to reflect on their priorities as if something had to be reset first before they could make further decisions. The shock of the lockdowns, the entire world simultaneously pressing the pause button, seems to have been so intense that individuals seemed ill at ease extracting themselves from the positions that had either been self-imposed or mandated by the State. Months later, as talks of what became known as the "Great Resignation" flooded the airwaves and the press; it increasingly felt that many had been traumatized by the pandemic while still ambivalent about what to make of it; knowing yet not knowing that the world would likely no longer be the same.

In fact, in the United States, states with the most new infections as the delta variant grew, such as Georgia, Florida and Louisiana, were the ones struggling the most finding workers willing to return to work. A record 4.4 million people, or 3 percent of the workforce quit in September 2021 following 4.3 million that had quit in August. Job seekers prioritized positions that allowed them to work remotely; an option that was not only perceived as increasing quality of life but more importantly provided protection from contamination. Collective behaviors that are first and foremost driven by psychosocial dynamics (e.g., anxieties and the social defenses mobilized in return) are also likely to be more resilient. As such, the labor shortage in evidence in the United States, the United Kingdom (also due to Brexit there), and now increasingly in Europe are unlikely to end anytime soon; supply chain disruptions taking a toll on several major economies and contributing to inflationary pressures. And yet, the "Great Resignation" terminology used to describe these phenomenal developments in the job market is not accurate. Rather than shunning work altogether, which is largely limited to those retiring earlier than they would otherwise have in the absence of the pandemic, what we are witnessing is shifting of priorities vis-à-vis work and even life in general. In essence what is happening in both the labor and the housing markets is quite similar in the sense that the observed behaviors in both situations are a reflection of significant shifts in priorities in response to social defenses mobilized against pandemic anxieties. There seems to be wishes of retreating into employment and/or housing situations that are capable of repairing the psychosocial onslaught brought upon by the pandemic through the provision of a nurturing space (more space, including outside) or work environment (increased flexibility and personal time). As is often the case, traumatic events at the societal level increase the propensity for individuals to shift their focus questioning and searching for renewed meaning, which in our view is what the sudden shifts in economic behaviors are precisely reflecting.

Furthermore, the psychosocial stress of the pandemic has led to another pandemic; that of individuals, no longer feeling "contained" by their own society and, as a consequence, acting out their frustration on others. This explains the bizarre rise in unruly and mask-less passengers on planes in the United States, the citizen's attacks on police in France, and the sharp rise in domestic violence worldwide. Sudden changes in the intensity and nature of societal level enactments, particularly those involving violence and/or a disavowal of the state's authority and/or societal norms, are crucial indicators of existing social defenses no longer able of containing the society.

In addition, while the young were largely spared from the hash realities of Covid-19 sickness, they seem to have been, especially early on, significantly impacted; preliminary research suggesting significant mental health consequences.[7] At the individual level, there is psychological distress, in particular with the youth that found itself isolated during its formative years. All of the above has led the Secretary General of the United Nations to call on nations to incorporate mental health services as an essential part of government responses to Covid-19. It is important to note that such recommended mental health actions would be at the individual level (i.e., micro) as opposed to the interventions at the societal level (i.e., macro) that are argued for here. See, Atlantic Currents (2021). The psychosocial mechanisms involving shared mental representations, fantasies, and defenses are not only quite different but also impossible to identify by just simply aggregating individual-level behaviors. Unconscious collusions are one of the main reasons behind this. See, Boccara (2014). Furthermore, the notions of individual and societal levels also differ. While this does not in any way discredit the validity of individual level mental health initiatives, the latter would not by themselves stave off potential serious societal level regressions in a variety of countries. It would therefore be a mistake, including at the theoretical level, to solely limit interventions at the micro level. This is sadly almost always the case; unconscious and conscious systems dynamics altogether ignored, in large part because of the misconception above.

Last, as alluded to earlier, the speed and intensity in which the real estate market changed in many parts of the world (e.g., China, Germany, New Zealand, Peru, United States) gives further credence to the idea that significant behavioral shifts, as a consequence once more of the psychosocial impact of the pandemic, are occurring with many individuals re-examining their lives. The sometimes-odd behaviors observed, akin to enactments such as paying twice the asking price, allowing sellers to remain in their property for an unusually long time after the sale is completed or even buying sellers a house so that they can sell theirs to the buyers suggest that panic, rather than rational economic decisions may have taken hold in some cases. This is another evidence suggesting that the pandemic must have been traumatic to many. Furthermore, for those less fortunate and, as such, not directly concerned by the overheated housing market, the pandemic only made life much harder by plunging many worldwide into poverty.

We are definitively in a time where psychosocial thinking to make sense of what we are witnessing is de rigueur. Therefore, understanding psychosocial issues that appear to already have had durable impacts on behaviors is paramount, especially as they also are key indicators of how future crises might be managed. However, there is nothing set in stone in the psychosocial dynamics that have been identified. Leadership almost always has an impact on the psychosocial dynamics. Of particular interest are whether or not leadership is reparative and the nature of its impact on empathic capability.

To this topic, we now turn in the chapter that follows.

NOTES

1. "Le Pr Montagnier apporte son soutien à la plainte pour l'arrêt de la vaccination de masse en Israël," *France Soir*, https://www.francesoir.fr/societe-sante/le-professeur-luc-montagnier-prix-nobel-amene-son-support-la-plainte-pour-larret-de-la, April 10, 2021.
2. See, https://www.youtube.com/watch?v=UVmXvo1FMOc, May 18, 2021.
3. "Vacationers shrug-off Covid-19 threat, flock to tourist destinations," *VN Express*, https://e.vnexpress.net/news/travel/places/vacationers-shrug-off-covid-19-threat-flock-to-tourist-destinations-4271361.html, May 2, 2021.
4. "The Hot-Person Vaccine," *The Atlantic*, https://www.theatlantic.com/technology/archive/2021/04/pfizer-gang-and-sadness-vaccine-culture/618755/, April 30, 2021.
5. "COVID-19: Bill Gates hopeful world 'completely back to normal' by end of 2022 and vaccine sharing to ramp up," *Sky News*, https://news.sky.com/story/covid-19-bill-gates-hopeful-world-completely-back-to-normal-by-end-of-2022-and-vaccine-sharing-to-ramp-up-12285840, April 25, 2020.
6. "Preserving intellectual property barriers to covid-19 vaccines is morally wrong and foolish," *Washington Post*, https://www.washingtonpost.com/opinions/2021/04/26/preserving-intellectual-property-barriers-covid-19-vaccines-is-morally-wrong-foolish/, April 26, 2020.
7. "51 percent of young Americans say they feel down depressed or hopeless," *CNBC*, https://www.cnbc.com/2021/05/10/51percent-of-young-americans-say-they-feel-down-depressed-or-hopeless.html, May 10, 2021.

Chapter 4

Leadership and Empathic Capability

INTRODUCTION

The previous two chapters focused on identifying the social defenses that were mobilized in a variety of countries at the onset of the pandemic and once vaccines became available. As is often the case, these social defenses hampered most countries' management of the pandemic. Yet, this does not have to be a foregone conclusion since social defenses do not have to be static over time. Country-level psychosocial work requires inputs from a variety of participants including constituents, media, government agencies, political actors, and academia. Leadership, in particular, can play a major role in enabling a society to work through its psychosocial issues. This, in turn, can have a major impact on the nature of the social defenses. In fact, the main purpose of working is precisely to decrease the propensity of regressed social defenses to be mobilized. To this, we now turn.

Moving forward, our hope is that leadership in several countries will start to systematically work with the relevant psychosocial data and allow its internalization. The latter is a prerequisite to leadership's capacity to enable societies to work-through their most salient psychosocial issues. While psychosocial work has yet to be undertaken at the country level under government management, it is important to remember that the work structure, if not its content and associative mode of operation, is already what takes place when societies debate public policies and social issues. The major difference is that psychosocial work takes into account explicitly how countries function as social systems, in particular the nature and purpose of the mostly unconscious social defenses mobilized against anxieties.

To illustrate what the suggestions above might entail, what follows highlights psychosocial aspects of leadership that are crucial in allowing societies to successfully manage crises such as the Covid-19 pandemic and its aftermath. We begin our inquiry by looking at Israel; a state whose performance went from the very best to what should have been avoided.

FROM ONE EXTREME TO THE NEXT IN ISRAEL

Throughout most of 2020, Deep Knowledge Group in Hong-Kong regularly assessed countries' management of the pandemic by evaluating quarantine efficiency, government management efficiency, monitoring and detection, and emergency treatment readiness. The State of Israel's management of the pandemic was consistently considered to be one of the best.[1] While this may no longer hold under the administration of Naftali Bennett, it does not impact the line of reasoning that follows.

Regardless of certain setbacks, albeit short-lived, the nation was particularly successful with its vaccination campaign that nations, all over the world, often sought to emulate it. Yet, as shown repeatedly over the course of the pandemic, almost no country was immune to renewed spikes in cases. This, for example, includes Israel, which had experienced four distinct waves by the Fall of 2021. While the last one surprised many since the country's population was highly vaccinated, the state responded swiftly by relying on booster doses, the very first country to do so, and managed to overcome what ended-up to be its worst wave without relying on any other restrictions. While the country ended-up suffering setbacks nevertheless, our focus in what follows is on the psychosocial dynamics that were observed in Israel at the onset of the pandemic.

Early developments in Israel did not augur well. Similarly to what was seen in London or New York, the Haredi community of ultra-orthodox Jews was slow to follow government directives and the infection spread rapidly. This, at first, seems counterintuitive since the health minister at the time, Yaakov Litzman, was himself a Haredi Jew. Furthermore, while Haredi communities are often perceived as deliberately refusing to embrace societal norms, there is nothing in the *Talmud* that goes against the adoption of safety precautions. In fact, quite the contrary as one of the most fundamental principles of Jewish Law, *pikuach nefesh*, is that human life always comes first.

I suspect that a long history of mistrust between the Haredi community, a symbolic "Other" par excellence, and the rest of the nation as well as paranoid projections in response to the danger that the invisible virus represented complicated the ability of the State to make itself heard by the Haredi community. Mental representations of the community, exacerbated by the fear in the general population that their conveniently found "malevolent" object would harbor and transmit the virus prevented "good enough" positive identification between opposing groups, which was required for a constructive empathetic dialogue to take place. The Minister himself, who incidentally contracted the virus along with his wife, may also have found it difficult to act in a community where authority lies exclusively with the rabbis. In addition, the Haredi community strongly believes that engaging in communal studies of the Torah is an affirmation of life; one rabbi indicating when the lockdown was announced that giving up studying the Torah was more dangerous than catching the virus. Last, as a consequence of their avoidance of the secular world, the community, less prone to watching the news, was not immediately aware of the lockdowns implemented by the authorities.

To be fair, the Israeli authorities had to manage taking into consideration the specificity of its Haredi community, a politically and culturally complex issue, while under extreme pressure to formulate and implement a program to address a rapidly evolving pandemic. The March 28, 2020, funeral in the community of Bnei Brak occurred 11 days after the government had implemented a full lockdown. The government understood all too well what the risks were and, as expected, this event turned into a major cluster of new infections. In fact, while the Haredi community represents only 12 percent of the Israeli population, it accounted early on for 60 percent of the infection and suffered from higher rates of mortality. Fortunately, a leading rabbi finally chose to ask his followers to self-isolate. As a consequence, while trust in the government remained low and the community remained suspicious of the Israeli police, the more so when it imposed large fines on those defying the lockdown, the situation ultimately evolved for the better.

But the story does not end here.

Psychosocially, the "Israel in the mind" can be characterized as "a Start-up company operating in a *Shtetl*."[2] As a social system, the hypothesis developed in Boccara (2014) is that it behaves as if it were besieged, terrified of abandonment and of annihilation but yet determined not to be "thrown back to the sea," whether by a virus or any other threatening object. Collective responses to survival anxieties have led to a high level of creativity, to discipline when necessary, and to benign and benevolent mental representations of institutions. As such, the population had full trust in the military and security services using their formidable logistical skills and sophisticated technology to fight the pandemic. Incidentally, unlike elsewhere, this did not even require consultation with the Knesset, the parliament. The Israelis were all too willing to have the two former institutions delivering them from the calamity that had befallen them. The results of the Israeli approach incorporating protective gestures, tracking, and testing served the country well. Thus, psychosocial dynamics do not have to systematically be an obstacle to policy making. The Israeli situation with Covid-19 highlights both a negative psychosocial impact on the ability and willingness of the Haredi community to accept and implement lockdown measures and a positive psychosocial impact on managing the pandemic efficiently. Ultimately, the psychosocial environment overall turned out to be a major help to the country's fighting of the pandemic. In an "all is well that ends well" moment, Israel emerged with impressive Covid-19 statistics. Sadly, in a harbinger of things to come nearly worldwide, Israel's impressive performance came to a screeching halt. Upon the emergence of the highly contagious omicron variant, the nation, in a bewildering complete U-turn, became one of the first to let go of the idea of containing the pandemic.

What is key is a country's ability to genuinely understand how it functions as a social system. And yet nothing suggests that this ability, in spite of psychoanalysis and psychosocial groups being well established in Israel, should be superior there than elsewhere. In fact, outside the pandemic, collectively confronting psychosocial dynamics in Israel is often met with difficult to breach resistance given the kind of geopolitical issues with which it is confronted. But for a collective threat such as the pandemic, the country romance, mental representations, and social defenses were all particularly well aligned in Israel to enable the nation to successfully address the pandemic and vaccination drive that followed.

The pandemic is a crisis of such magnitude that it has the capacity to shock social systems to the point of reconfiguring social defenses. Depending on whether or not it becomes an opportunity for working through salient psychosocial issues, the resulting changes in psychosocial dynamics could be for the better or for the worse. Sadly, in the case of Israel, the pandemic did not translate into a reset and strengthened relationship with the Palestinians. Not trying to increase availability of vaccines to the West Bank was probably a missed opportunity. Yet, Palestinian medical personnel from Gaza received training in Israel. This is noteworthy as Hamas not only sanctioned it but the Palestinian Authority in the West Bank was also, unlike what would have been standard procedure, bypassed. This suggests direct—while discreet—engagement between Hamas and Israelis, even if violence and mistrust have, as recent developments clearly showed, certainly not abated. Furthermore, the pandemic also created opportunities for cooperation between Israel and the United Arab Emirates on technology transfer. And Hamas is not alone.

A SHORT NOTE FROM KABUL TO BOGOTA

In Afghanistan, months before seizing power, the Taliban had already launched a public-health awareness campaign educating people on hygiene, the use of protective equipment, and the adoption of social distancing. It also set up quarantine sites and instructed people not to visit mosques. Thus, in a move reminiscent of what are long standing practices for Hezbollah in Lebanon, the Taliban positioned itself as a group capable of assuming public service responsibilities in areas where the State was unable to fulfill that role.[3] While the Taliban was almost surely engaging in moves aimed at benefitting them, this could possibly, notwithstanding the huge psychosocial shock brought by the US's decision to completely pull out of Afghanistan, encourage a process of changing mental representations within Afghanistan and create opportunities on all sides for reintegration into civilian life. A postscript on Afghanistan and the Taliban was added after this paragraph was written. The reasons for doing so are given in the preamble to the postscript.

In an unexpected twist, Jihadist groups have also used the pandemic as a rallying cry. The pandemic fed perfectly into the narrative that governments were indifferent to the wellbeing of their population. That message aligned well with the rejection of the State amongst marginalized populations in regions, for example the Sahel in West Africa, where Jihadist groups are particularly active. While Western scientists pondered the origins of the virus, Islamist insurgents viewed it as God's wrath destined at punishing the infidels/crusaders. Yet, they have not offered ideas nor launched initiatives to address the pandemic. The frustrations, increased time spent on social medias during the pandemic, and undoing wishes also relevant to a marginalized and defiant youth may all favor recruitment efforts by Jihadist groups.

The situation in Colombia, another country beset by internal conflicts, was far more complex due to the multitude of insurgency groups there. While the National Liberation Army (ELN), a leftist insurgency group, had initially proposed a ceasefire, it was only short-lived. Violence by the ELN and other insurgency groups, including killings of citizens simply for not respecting Covid-19 lockdowns, occurred in many communities.[4] Sadly, the situation continuously worsened on both the public health and the political front.[5] This was not expected since Colombian institutions have traditionally been very strong. The combination of social discontent that was responded to with unusually harsh violence from the Duque administration and of huge scars from the civil war with social leaders and former insurgents that have reintegrated society often being killed all happening during the worst phase of the Covid-19 crisis greatly complicated the management of the pandemic in Colombia. The lockdowns that were imposed initially, when the pandemic was much less virulent, were all eliminated at its height. While lockdowns are much harder to maintain in countries with a larger segment of the population living at the subsistence level, there is nevertheless a widespread belief, especially among the young and the left, that lockdowns were timed to shut down antigovernment protests, and that the pandemic was used to try to pass unpopular legislation while the population's attention was diverted.

Unsurprisingly, empathic availability will almost always be in short supply in regions beset by intractable conflicts. However, it is absolutely essential to successfully incorporate psychosocial and systems dynamics into public policy. We now address this by surveying the developments at the onset of the pandemic in Belgium, the State of Kerala in India, and New Zealand.

REPARATIVE LEADERSHIP AND NARCISSISTIC WITHDRAWAL

Belgium is an interesting case as it holds the unenviable record of having had one the highest number of Covid-19 deaths per capita; exceeding 2000 per million as of May 2021. To make matters worse, with the Flemish and French speaking regions at loggerhead for years over the direction that the country should take, Belgium was only able to form a caretaker government a few months before the Covid-19 pandemic with Minister Wilmes at the helm; an individual until then completely unknown to most. When the pandemic hit, all political parties agreed to give the government special powers to bypass the legislative process. As a consequence, Sophie Wilmes, the first female prime minister in the history of Belgium, found herself in charge of the worst crisis the country had faced since World War II; a rather odd situation as the majority of Belgians were not even aware that she had been prime minister since October. And yet, the prime minister, whose nickname "*Super Sophie*" speaks volumes concerning the way she has been perceived, quickly gained the confidence of the Belgian public through her pragmatism and humility. While she bore the brunt of the anger and resentment of many of the health workers, she also won high praise for her management of the pandemic. This is no small feat in a highly polarized country with, at the time, the worst Covid-19 mortality in the world. Sadly, under the leadership of Prime Minister De Croo, Belgium found itself unable to manage the pandemic well, in large part because of rigid and blind faith in its sanitary pass (*CST*) and the resulting exclusion—through discrimination—of the unvaccinated. France and Italy embarked on similar paths.

The counter intuitive mental developments above immediately bring to mind the flurry of press articles about women-led nations performing better than others in managing the pandemic. While this seems to be the case, witness the experiences of Taiwan, South Korea, Iceland, Denmark, and Finland, many countries with male leaders, for example Vietnam, Greece, and Australia also did well overall, even if each of those three countries experienced setbacks. While gender of the leader may seem to matter, it is likely to be more a reflection of a society's inclusiveness, hence of its ability to work with different constituencies. But what genuinely matters from a psychosocial and systems dynamics perspective is the notion of reparative leadership. It emphasizes reflectiveness, shared meaning, and empathic availability at the level of the entire society. These attributes, which are the hallmark of country-level psychosocial thinking and inquiry, cut across gender. While internalized representations of gender roles influenced by culture, gender-influenced projections onto leaders and what, in turn, gets introjected by them may all decrease the propensity of male leaders to be reparative, this does not have to be the case. Socio-Analytic Dialogue's central premise is that leadership can become reparative if it is willing and able to promote both citizen's internalization of how their country functions as a social system and positive identification between subgroups in society.

What Covid-19 revealed through the failures of leaders such as Donald Trump in the United States, Jair Bolsonaro in Brazil, or Narendra Modi in India is that promoting the mobilization of regressed social defenses while managing the pandemic is likely to fail. Sadly, while the Trump administration deserves credit for Operation Warp Speed's incredible success at enabling an unusually fast development of vaccines, everything on the fight against Covid-19 was sabotaged by adverse psychosocial dynamics that were encouraged by the same administration. With a pandemic, there was no designated enemy that could defensively be scapegoated or silenced. The need to restore containment at the group level created a need for objects of idealization, which is how first line responders were initially perceived throughout most of the world. Successful management of the pandemic likely required those objects, in the role of protective figures, to also be located within governments, which turned out to be the case in Germany with Angela Merkel. Reparative leaders can create a degree of connectedness that is otherwise absent once a society faces Covid-19 as a traumatic experience. This is crucial since it comes precisely at a point in time when the society requires it. On the other hand, failure to connect to a "good" (aka reassuring) leader ultimately leads to the reawakening of archaic anxieties and to paranoid regression. Morality and norms are then bound to weaken similarly to what is observed in societies when large group identity is under threat. See, Volkan (2006).

Another interesting case is that of Kerala state in India. The southern state, known for its outstanding social policy and indicators, initially managed extremely well and counted only 4 deaths at the end of May 2020 for a population of 35 million. As soon as the health minister there, K. K. Shailaja, heard about the epidemic in Wuhan, Kerala started to meticulously prepare for what they foresaw could happen. It readied itself to implement all the World Health Organization's recommendations on testing, tracing, and isolating even before it had its first case at the end of January; a passenger returning from Wuhan. The health minister, a former high school science teacher born into a family of activists, fondly nicknamed the "Coronavirus Slayer" stands out for her simple demeanor. I believe that the key factor behind her early success is her extraordinary capacity for narcissistic withdrawal. This is a quality that would become increasingly valued were societies to choose incorporating psychosocial thinking into public policy and dialogue. Narcissistic withdrawal often translates into a genuine availability to listen to others as well as a capacity to focus on goals without being hampered or distracted by personal considerations (e.g., search for narcissistic gratification).

Narcissistic withdrawal can be harder to maintain the longer one has been in power. This is why Socio-Analytic Dialogue consistently emphasizes working psychosocially. Doing so enables societies' cultural emphasis to increasingly shift toward promoting and enabling the kind of leadership discussed above.

In New Zealand, Jacinda Ardern's unique capacity to credibly emphasize society-level empathy, something already in evidence in the aftermath of the Christchurch terrorist attack, had an extraordinary impact on the country's management of Covid-19. The measures taken were decisive, implemented quickly and early, and, most importantly, empathetically explained to the general population. As a consequence, New Zealand was not only able to flatten the curve but also at first to essentially eliminate the virus altogether. While facilitated by the country's remoteness and high level of basic trust, this is truly an extraordinary achievement. It makes New Zealand's prime minister probably the most effective leader today. This is, however, not something that came as a surprise. In fact, a Socio-Analytic Dialogue blog, Kia Ora "Economics of Kindness" published in January 2019,[6] had already singled out her leadership qualities. As is also discussed in a blog published by NIODA in Australia,[7] New Zealand has been the closest to reparative leadership. Through the promotion of empathic availability and search for meaning, which reduces societal splitting, the country's leadership has achieved something that few politicians are willing and able to do. Yet, even there, the public policy framework reflected by the adoption of a wellbeing budget, called an "Economics of Kindness," was not and could not (it relied on fiscal tools alone) transform the society psychosocially. While this may not be a constraint right now in New Zealand, no country is immune to psychosocial shocks. While New Zealand was lucky to have Jacinda Ardern at the helm as it faced the pandemic, the only way to render a country, including New Zealand, psychosocially robust enough to face whatever shocks it may face in the future is to formalize the adoption of a rigorous framework rather than rely on the personality of a specific leader.

We now contrast those experiences with that of two leaders, Donald Trump and Narendra Modi, for whom the psychosocial dynamics were such that leadership was anything but reparative.

DESTRUCTIVE LEADERSHIP

As is well known, Trump was excessively driven by his ego at the expense of almost everything else. Uncomfortable at being challenged, he could not admit being wrong and was prone to surround himself with individuals with unshakable loyalty to him. This often led to poor decision-making; something that became all too apparent during his failed management of Covid-19. In his quest to be adulated by his constituents, he often distorted facts, denied the pandemic by repeatedly attempting to undo it, and encouraged the nation to eschew collective efforts in fighting it. As deaths skyrocketed, his lack of empathy prevented him from changing course. As a polarizing figure, many loathed him. Yet, the psychosocial dynamics that he encouraged were nevertheless very much anchored in the social fabric of the country. The "Make America Great Again" social system, in its futile attempts to restore an omnipotence fantasy in the face of an event it could not address without humility, met a challenge it could not overcome.

This was, for example, in evidence early on with the way his administration handled the debate on the origins of the pandemic. As we referred to earlier, allegations that the virus could have been inadvertently released from the Wuhan lab were made on several occasions. Yet, Trump's administration chose to ignore these. While referring to Covid-19 as the "China virus," it never attempted to investigate whether the virus might have originated in a laboratory. While psychosocially explosive, the allegations regained traction following a Wall Street Journal report citing declassified intelligence that staff from the Wuhan research laboratory staffs had fallen ill with symptoms mimicking what is now known about Covid-19 as early as November 2019.[8] But, while the Trump administration would have had an incentive in an election year in trying to shed light on this, it was not even attempted. Trump did not have the credibility to do so in light of his distorting facts often for political purposes and rejecting inconvenient truths whenever it suited him. Thus, how psychosocial dynamics influenced Trump's leadership may not only have hurt him politically but also prevented deeper collaboration with China to better understand, hence manage, the pandemic.

In the case of the United States, the big pharmaceutical companies have long hijacked public health policy. As such, the nation was particularly prone to conspiracy theories. The latter fulfilled a defensive role since fear of the pandemic could be substituted by a disavowal of a system experienced as deliberately stoking that fear as a way to bring a totalitarian state. Although seemingly farfetched, similar ideas got traction elsewhere; an indication of the profound malaise—independently of the pandemic—increasingly taking hold all over the world. As always, understanding the underlying anxieties is a prerequisite to understanding and working with the social defenses mobilized against those anxieties. Experiencing the pandemic as a conspiracy had meaning since it reflected—in displacement—the disavowal of a system that is fast losing all credibility.

Alternatively, the situation in China stands in sharp contrast with that of the United States since the country has consistently maintained its strict adherence to a "zero Covid" strategy. While the rest of the world may already have lost its battle with Covid-19, the disease having become endemic; the Chinese authorities are finding themselves in a bind since their credibility rests on strictly maintaining that policy. The authorities' message has consistently been that the successful eradication of Covid-19 in China, independently of the collective sacrifice that it entailed, demonstrated the superiority of the Chinese centralized governance approach. A majority of Chinese, whose social system still "remembers" the poverty and humiliation of its still recent past, were all too eager to accept the sacrifices that the Chinese authorities demanded in exchange for the societal containment provided by the "zero Covid" strategy. As such, the Chinese, possibly experiencing the closing of the country to the outside world as a repair act akin to a rebirth to times when the nation was the most preeminent in the world—have until now neither resisted the continued closing of the country to the outside world nor the increased concentration of power amongst the top echelon of the communist party.

A core lesson is that empathic availability is an absolute prerequisite worldwide to face crises of the magnitude that we are seeing now. While whether a given leader is empathetic or not remains a function of that leader's psychological make up, it is undeniable that empathic availability does not exist in a vacuum. It is instead also very much influenced by the social system. On that front, as discussed in the section on the United States, psychosocial dynamics worldwide are promoting, thanks to narcissism and obsession with personal gratification, a retreat away from empathy. This is, therefore, very much something whose promotion in societies worldwide should be urgently prioritized. We return to this important topic in chapter 7.

This failure in leadership is however not limited to the United States. It was also on display in India, not to mention Brazil; two countries that share many similarities with the experience of the United States under Trump.

What happened in India with the pandemic is also directly connected to Modi's leadership. Similarly to Trump, Modi has prioritized image over substance. Modi's attempts at psychosocial repair acts have gone even further than Trump's "Make America Great Again" in its exclusion of minorities that do not fit the idealized mental representations of India's Hindu heritage. In doing so, he has purportedly encouraged violence and promoted grandiose construction projects. The latter included a 2.8 billion US dollars construction project to build a new parliament building, the prime minister's residence and other government buildings in central Delhi. The grandiose construction project was considered essential and, as such, continued during the pandemic while the capital city and the rest of the nation were experiencing serious equipment shortages, notably lifesaving oxygen tanks. While hugely popular by focusing, albeit perversely and dangerously, on Hindu identity, Modi's handling of the pandemic has increasingly triggered unprecedented criticism of the Prime Minister, including by some of its most ardent supporters.

As is well known, the situation in India has been catastrophic; oxygen in short supply, bodies piling up faster in cremation sites than workers could build new pyres, and seemingly countless unreported deaths in the rural areas. Images of thousands of bodies floating up the river Ganges truly shocked the world. And yet, in spite of all of this, the Indian administration continued to focus more on managing its image, intimidating the media in the process, rather than tackling the pandemic. And yet, unlike Trump or Bolsonaro, Modi never downplayed the virus and took it seriously. Maybe even too seriously! A strict national lockdown was imposed with less than four hours notice, stranding millions of migrant workers all over India. Furthermore, as in so many countries, the Indian administration in an effort to undo the pandemic and in response to shared wishes that it could end, reopened the country too quickly. In a nation with the population density that India has, this turned out to be a fatal mistake. Besides packed cricket matches, notably in Modi's home state of Gujarat, the nail in the coffin was—as we already mentioned-the Kumbh Mela festival that attracted millions of pilgrims without any social distancing in Haridwar on the river Ganges.

As is almost always the case, enactments in the name of national identity can be quite deadly. While there was no civil war in this particular instance (the condition in which social defenses mobilized in the name of preserving large group identity are at their most regressed), the gatherings of large crowds promoted by Modi's in the name of religion or of politics (BJP election rallies) also proved to be deadly. As voting was closing in Bengal, the positivity rate was estimated to be 50 percent in Kolkata.[9] Similarly to what was observed with Trump's political rallies in Oklahoma, the political meetings that were encouraged in Modi's India also led to super spreader events. In fact, India's population density assured that the events would create a medical catastrophe on a scale never seen before.

Once again, leadership catastrophically failed its people due to psychosocial dynamics, particularly those pertaining to national identity, which hijacked public decisions. The scale at which this took place in India defies comprehension. In the words of Indian writer, Arundhati Roy, "it is a crime against humanity."[10] With the country focused on its vaccination drive, 1 billion doses administered by late October 2021, and a likely a large share of its population having been exposed to the virus, the country seemed able to overcome the catastrophic developments and manage.

Another example of destructive leadership includes Brazil's Jair Bolsonaro who consistently downplayed the severity of the virus, including when he was himself diagnosed with Covid-19. As such, he always remained defiant in his systematic rejection of mitigating measures (e.g., lockdowns, masks, social distancing). In spite of both their leaders being populists, the situations of India and of Brazil are quite different since Modi recognized the seriousness of the pandemic while Bolsonaro always refused to do so. In the risk of oversimplifying, Modi's policy response was probably hijacked by social defenses mobilized in response to the wish to assert national identity (at least a Hindu version) while Bolsonaro's response was outright denial. Both leaders, as observed nearly everywhere else, wished for an undoing whose enactment turned out to be extraordinarily costly to their respective countries. As is almost always the case, their wishes might also have been, at least partially, a response to what the society would have projected (or deposited) onto them through unconscious communications between the society and its leader.

A country that defied expectations is Chile, which experienced a significant surge in Covid-19 cases despite what had been a well-managed vaccination program; the country benefitting from one of the highest vaccination rates in the world. This could be due to the extreme divisions that the country has struggled with. Some have accused the authorities of having been caught in triumphalism, notably by opening the external borders too quickly at the onset of the Southern hemisphere summer and encouraging Chileans to travel around the country during that period. Yet something deeper must also be at play. As argued in a psychosocial analysis of the post-Pinochet Chilean transition to a more pluralistic society, Chileans have very little trust in their institutions; basic trust much lower than it should be in a nation at its level of economic development and success. See, Boccara (2014). At a deeper psychosocial level, there exists in Chile a significant ambivalence about success, due to the fact that the nation was never able to fully mourn its past due to the circumstances under which Pinochet relinquished power.[11] While the latter applies first and foremost to economic success, the nation missed the opportunity to leverage its well-organized public health system to establish contact-tracing protocols and better inform its population concerning the nature of the disease. This suggests that ambivalence might have also played a role in the implementation of public health policies. The pandemic occurred at a time when the nation was gripped with major protests in anticipation of the October 2020 popular referendum to create a Constituent Assembly and the May 2021 election of the latter.[12] As a consequence, the government had very low credibility. The distrust that the majority of the population had of the right-wing Pinera administration significantly complicated the latter's messaging and risk management.

We now turn to France, a nation where leadership found itself hampered in it's the management of the pandemic.

UNRESOLVED CONFLICTS AND EXCEPTIONALISM IN FRANCE

At the onset of the summer of 2021, Western Europe seemed on the brink of having successfully managed the pandemic through a combination of public health policies limiting the spread of the virus and vaccination. Once policy decisions were taken, implementation, albeit uneven, was sufficiently thought through for the public health policies to reach their objectives. Yet in France, a country where the number of cases and deaths per capita has been one of the worst in Western Europe, the authorities seemed to have insufficiently taken into account how mental representations of the leadership and of the nation impacted public health policies.

Mental representations of the leadership, especially the head of state, matter. They must be understood and taken into account when designing and implementing public policies. They can influence how a specific policy will be perceived and, as such, have an impact on its implementation. While Jacinda Ardern in New Zealand found herself able to make the country receptive to implementation of strict measures, Emmanuel Macron of France may have suffered from a leadership deficit that hampered France's management of the pandemic.

France entered the pandemic period in a tense social atmosphere due to unmet social demands and anger at the government. As in any social system, the more so if it finds itself beset by a high level of anxieties, France's policy responses to the pandemic should have taken into account more seriously the nature and intensity of the social defenses mobilized at the time; in other words, ways in which the country functioned as a social system.

The yellow jackets (*Gilets Jaunes*) movement not only laid bare the profound level of discontent in the country but also the prevalence of latent, albeit at times acted-out, aggression. Disillusioned after a brief period of idealization of a President whose movement, *En Marche*, had been portrayed as having overcome the traditional divisions that characterized France, the latent aggression morphed into a visceral hatred of President Macron. Unsuccessful at the reparative leadership role that France had hoped for, the President quickly became in the eyes of the public an envied object representative of the perverse elites who had despoiled those left behind by the system. As often turns out to be the case in those situations, this led to a weakening of basic trust. The latter is frequently a precursor to violence. Latent aggression does not, however, imply that French society is incapable of displaying an impressive level of social conscience and solidarity; in fact, quite the opposite as shown by the many sacrifices that citizens were willing to make during the lockdowns. Yet, as could be seen almost daily and certainly during the numerous strikes, the ways in which individuals in France interact with one another can be fraught with contempt and aggression. This was, for example, the case with the May 2021 series of attacks (knife, lone shooters) against the police. Incidentally, I believe that it is the most important psychosocial characteristic behind the country's well-known sense of gloom. And yet as a reflection of social defenses denying aggression and its influence on the country's mood, a majority of the French might nevertheless still react to such assessments with derision.

The threat and the shock of the pandemic allowed several of the psychosocial mechanisms alluded to above to remain hidden, albeit not far from the surface. While the French public respected the lockdown measures relatively well, the latter, however, had to be accompanied by strict enforcement measures. Venturing outside one's home required the completion of a form that was only valid once and police checks were frequent and infractions systematically met by fines. In an odd move perhaps indicative of the French public's ambivalent attitude towards the State, French news seemed to delight in airing stories of individuals cheating on the lockdowns. The casual rather than incriminating tone used suggests that beating the system was likely experienced as a badge of honor as would be the case with a scoring game.

In an address standing for its stark opposition in style to that adopted by either Angela Merkel or Jacinda Ardern in mandating a lockdown, President Macron's stern announcement of France's lockdown mentioned, "We are at War" several times during an intervention that only lasted twenty minutes. He not only positioned himself as a de Gaulle-like commander in chief but also as a benevolent yet condescending figure calling on the French people to spend the time "reading, reflecting on what is essential." This stance, although presidential and meant to be reassuring, was risky for a president who did not benefit from the same level of trust as did Merkel or Ardern did; the French President far from being an object of positive identification at the time.

The *coup de grâce* though came when the authorities reversed the official guidelines on personal protective equipment. The situation on masks resembled that of the United States discussed earlier. After insisting for weeks that it was not necessary for the general public, pharmacies even forbidden to sell them, the government announced that masks were absolutely essential (though shying away from making them compulsory as the French Academy of Medicine had advocated) and would, as such, be available soon. Rather than explaining that there was a shortage in France (something all medical personnel knew and said), the authorities were seen as having maliciously duped the French population into a false and dangerous sense of safety. As masks suddenly flooded the market, the general public wondering where they all suddenly came from, it then became the medical personnel's turn to feel cheated since they had endured unsafe working conditions because of the lack of protective equipment. This *affaire des masques* turned out to be a serious blunder on the part of the French authorities. Early on, facemasks "in the mind" had become the vehicle through which to express collective wishes for a benevolent and protective government; in other words, for the missing reparative leadership that had been hoped for after the election of President Macron. Thus, while there was a shortage, the facemask became, in displacement, an object of desire. However, in a *volte-face* typical of French's casual attitudes towards State imposed measures, it ceased to be desired once it became available. For many, the deliberate refusal to wear facemasks or practice social distancing became a way to disavow, once more in displacement, the State.

Sadly, France had an unusually hard time containing the pandemic. Ultimately, its performance was one of the worse in Europe. It had the highest number of cases besides Russia, a much larger nation straddling two continents, as well as one of the highest numbers of deaths in Europe. Delaying necessary lockdowns meant that restrictions ended up having to be imposed for much longer and, therefore, at a greater cost. This highlights once more that psychosocial dynamics can have hugely important behavioral consequences. The traditional distrust and, as a result, confrontational relationship that exist in France towards the State in its role of enforcer of laws and norms was exacerbated by its lack of constancy during the management of the pandemic. While the authorities understood that enforcement mechanisms involving police checks and monetary fines would be necessary, those also backfired. Disempowered and infantilized by the strict controls, French residents never genuinely embraced the idea of adhering to a collective national effort against the pandemic. Social defenses mobilized to rebel against the authority of the State prevented that. This is disheartening as, unlike the United States, France is often more than ready—as has regularly been the case throughout its history—to embrace solidarity and act on it. In fact, this is one of the defining psychosocial characteristics of its social system. But it was not the case this time around. Unsurprisingly, the disavowal of the State was expressed through weekly demonstrations all over the country against the *pass sanitaire*, a document showing proof of vaccination or of a recent negative test in order to be able to access most public spaces. This disappearance of basic trust following the ways in which several governments, including France, managed because of the lack of sufficient transparency and changing goal posts (e.g., third booster) was a serious drawback. At least, the French authorities were able to impose the public health measures mentioned above while the United States laissez faire attitude resulted in the country finding itself falling behind after a strong start, relatively to others, in its vaccination coverage. This can only facilitate the potential emergence of vaccine resistant strains. Ambivalence towards President Macron and the State coupled with actions that generated mistrust of the authorities may have led to some not protecting themselves and others from the virus as a way to express defiance at the lack of sufficiently reparative leadership. As a disavowal of, if not an attack on, the State and the President, this may have led to medical consequences that might have otherwise been avoided. It seemed once again to be the case with France's fourth wave that started in July 2021 since new cases once more greatly exceeded that of other European countries. Once again, analyzing psychosocial dynamics and the ways in which they influence communications, whether on public policies or between government and its constituents, is absolutely essential.

Another area where France's psychosocial dynamics hampered its management of the pandemic is public schooling. As is almost always the case, public policies that are experienced as conflicting with the ways in which national identity is defined and experienced are often resisted upon. France's identity is embedded in the provision of free and standardized schooling to all children of the republic. As such, there was an extreme reluctance, again as a policy experienced as an attack on identity, to close schools. The fact that it was known that school children could catch the virus and spread it at home was systematically denied. The cost turned out to be quite high. For example, in one school in the department of Seine St Denis near Paris, twenty pupils lost family members to what is thought to have been in home contamination brought from school.[13] For France, a country that often needs as the expression of a social defense to distinguish itself from the rest of Europe, maintaining schools open was a point of pride that positively differentiated the country from the rest of its neighbors. France closed its schools for 10 weeks against 35 in Italy, 28 in Germany, and 27 in the UK. The fear in egalitarian France was that some kids would be left behind. As such, right when neighboring Italy closed its own schools, the French Minister of European Affairs tweeted, "Amid the comparisons, let's not forget what works and what we pride ourselves on: No other country in the European Union has left its schools open as much as France has."[14] But schools in poorer neighborhoods had greater difficulties maintaining the safety protocols required. In fact, an

English teacher in the school in Seine Saint Denis mentioned earlier had also reported how in some schools in the poorer suburbs, windows did not even open, pupils were reluctant to keep their masks on (difficult to enforce), and hygiene was lacking. Similarly to defending the refusal to close school on psychological grounds (e.g., no pupils should be left behind, issues of fairness), a lockdown strongly recommended by the medical community in early January 2021 was vetoed by President Macron on the grounds that lockdowns were dangerous on mental health grounds. Yet fear of Covid-19 was likely taking a greater mental toll on the population. Macron, gearing up for his presidential campaign, was therefore willing to sacrifice public health in the name of not alienating his electorate. As it turns out, it was a risky gamble that may nevertheless have been shrewd on his part, notwithstanding the rapid spread of the delta variant, as it seems to have paid off with France's ability to accelerate its vaccination campaign before the summer of 2021. But vaccines for teachers were not sufficiently available at the time schools reopened. While many have strongly criticized maintaining schools open while it was known that children were a vector of transmission, the government defended its position by saying that it could not compromise on children's education.

And last, as in many other countries, the pandemic in France led to an increase in poverty, loneliness, psychological issues and educational difficulties. Furthermore, in what would be appear to be an odd development, notwithstanding the fact both Presidents Francois Mitterand and Charles de Gaulle consulted astrologist, a lot of French youth turned to astrology during the pandemic. Anxieties should never be underestimated. Thus, as illustrated by a psychosocial and systems dynamics understanding of France, the leadership there became hostage to negative projections and basic trust eroded. However, after a catastrophic start, the authorities were able to significantly change course through the early adoption of a *Pass Sanitaire*. The French public not only supported it in a large majority but also responded, the true purpose of the policy, by increasing vaccine intake.

The previous paragraphs on France were all written in May 2021, hence prior to the country being once again at the forefront worldwide of the worsening situation with the omicron variant. Furthermore, the increased splitting against unvaccinated individuals deliberately encouraged by President Emmanuel Macron[15] and included in the January 2021 law on *Pass Vaccinal* highlights the propensity of France—as a social system—to mobilize regressed social defenses. Unsurprisingly, all that was written psychosocially a few months ago still applies. The underlying psychosocial issues are unlikely to be collectively worked through in the absence of the authorities incorporating psychosocial analysis into their public policy framework. The unchanged and rigid nature of France' social defenses against anxieties illustrates perfectly the relevance and explanatory power of the psychosocial dynamics thinking underpinning the book. The same could be said about many other nations, particularly at a time when a large part the world appears to be once and for all ready to consider endemicity of Covid-19 a foregone conclusion.

CONCLUSIONS

This chapter has illustrated ways in which mental representations, level of anxieties, nature of defenses mobilized against those anxieties, and other psychosocial dynamics (e.g., influence of history and culture) all played a significant role in determining how each country faced the pandemic. Yet, all the countries faced the same event more or less at the same time. As such, unsurprisingly the anxieties were also similar and the social defenses, if and when mobilized, shared some similarities. Wishing for an undoing was widely shared. However, how to achieve the latter varied across nations. This is because the degree of social solidarity, hence the willingness and ability to sacrifice something on behalf of others, considerably differed. Overall, it appears the social defenses hampered managing the pandemic the most whenever issues related to national identity surfaced.

NOTES

1. See, https://www.express.co.uk/travel/articles/1270421/coronavirus-safest-countries-in-the-world-crisis-management-deep-knowledge-group-analysis, accessed May 1, 2021. Since then, Deep Knowledge Group has begun to assess cities instead and Tel Aviv is ranked high due to its innovative vaccination strategy (targeting hard to reach communities and working on vaccine hesitancy). See, https://www.dka.global/covid-city-ranking, accessed June 15, 2021.

2. See, Chapter 2, section 4 of Boccara (2014).

3. "The Afghan Taliban and Covid-19: Leveraging the Crisis or a Change of Heart," *Middle East Institute Publications*, See, https://www.mei.edu/publications/afghan-taliban-and-covid-19-leveraging-crisis-or-change-heart, April 13, 2021.

4. "Colombia: Armed Groups' Brutal Covid Measures," *Human Rights Watch*, https://www.hrw.org/news/2020/07/15/colombia-armed-groups-brutal-covid-19-measures#, July 15, 2020.

5. "Everything is Collapsing: Colombia battles third Covid wave amid unrest," *The Guardian*, https://www.theguardian.com/global-development/2021/jun/22/colombia-covid-coronavirus-third-wave-unrest, June 22, 2021.

6. See, https://socioanalyticdialogue.org/blog/kia_ora_economics_of_kindness, January 28, 2019.

7. See, https://www.nioda.org.au/reparative-leadership-in-2020/, February 10, 2020. NIODA is a groundbreaking non-profit organization located in Melbourne that provides education, research, coaching, and consultancy in organizational dynamics.

8. "Wuhan lab staff sought hospital care before COVID-19 outbreak disclosed –WSJ," *Reuters*, https://www.reuters.com/business/healthcare-pharmaceuticals/wuhan-lab-staff-sought-hospital-care-before-covid-19-outbreak-disclosed-wsj-2021-05-23/, May 23, 2021.

9. "Every second person getting tested in Kolkata is positive," *Times of India*, https://timesofindia.indiatimes.com/city/kolkata/every-second-person-getting-tested-in-kolkata-is-positive/articleshow/82236519.cms, April 25, 2021.

10. "We are witnessing a crime against humanity: Arundhati Roy on India's Covid catastrophe," *The Guardian*, https://www.theguardian.com/news/2021/apr/28/crime-against-humanity-arundhati-roy-india-covid-catastrophe, April 28, 2021.

11. Pinochet resigned but stayed on as senator for life. While the dictatorship brought significant hardships and human rights violation, economic performance was overall strong, notwithstanding early mistakes and the significant burden imposed on the poorer segments of the society. As such, there has always been an ambivalence surrounding success. See, Boccara (2014), Chapter 5.

12. The Chilean Constitution had essentially remained unchanged since the Pinochet dictatorship and the referendum and election of a Constituent Assembly was widely seen as absolutely essential to address the long-standing fractures of Chilean society and to decrease corruption and inequalities.

13. "France kept classrooms open 'at all costs.' At a school where 20 pupils lost loved ones, some say the price was too high," *CNN*, https://www.cnn.com/2021/05/04/europe/france-school-deaths-covid-cmd-intl/index.html, May 4, 2021.

14. "A French exception: Experts call for rethink of open-schools policy amid pandemic," *France 24*, https://www.france24.com/en/europe/20210317-a-french-exception-pride-and-regret-over-france-s-open-schools-amid-pandemic, March 17, 2021.

15. "Emmanuel Macron: « je veux emmerder les non-vaccinées », des propos qui passent mal" *France Info*, https://www.francetvinfo.fr/sante/maladie/coronavirus/pass-sanitaire/emmanuel-macron-je-veux-emmerder-les-non-vaccines-des-propos-qui-passent-mal_4905281.html, January 5, 2022.

Chapter 5

From Psychosocial Extinction to Psychosocial Renewal

This chapter is an important transition chapter as it shifts the focus from the pandemic to future systemic crises that humanity is expected to face. As stated from the very beginning, the book's purpose is to advocate for a systematic and embedded psychosocial and systems dynamics approach to public policy and country dialogue. As chapters 2 through 4 have shown, unacknowledged and misunderstood psychosocial dynamics ended-up significantly hampering the management of the pandemic almost everywhere. Unless worked through, perverse societal dynamics, a sense of entitlement buttressed by narcissistic greed, and last but not least social defenses similar to those identified during the pandemic are likely to also hamper humanity's ability to successfully—and collectively—face future systemic crises.

A society's inability to work through its own psychosocial issues is likely to lead to the mobilization of further regressed social defenses that can only increase the likelihood of public policies failing to meet their objectives. Thus, the chapter argues that societies should focus on doing their utmost to avoid what is referred to as psychosocial extension. With the latter, meaning gets lost once the capacity to work through has been destroyed. Societies should, therefore, strive to work towards what is referred to as psychosocial renewal whereas that capacity to work through is instead continuously strengthened.

TIGERS AT THE GATE

"Tigers at the Gate" is the title that Christopher Fry chose for his translation of Giraudoux's "*La guerre de Troie n'aura pas lieu*" play into English. The French play, which premiered in Paris in 1935 is a criticism of the leadership's response to the psychosocial dynamics that Giraudoux understood as not only having led to World War I but also as likely leading to another catastrophic conflict. However, few were capable of genuinely hearing what Giraudoux was warning them of at the time. But yet, the impending doom should have been apparent to those in the nineteen thirties who repeatedly witnessed grotesque displays of nationalism, massive rallies such as those immortalized by Riefenstahl's "Triumph of the Will," and countless individuals eagerly repudiating their old values. Unfortunately, such collective denials have repeated themselves throughout history. This suggests that the observed phenomenon may very well be an intrinsic part of human nature. This was the conclusion reached in a Jerusalem Post article, arguing that World War II could have been avoided with, "when the 'writing on the wall' says that danger is at our doorstep, the human race refuses to read it, and instead enlists its intelligence to create an 'alternative story' which won't require it to take drastic steps."[1]

As history has shown, humanity has often paid dearly for its collective denials. But maybe this time, history will be kinder to us. With humanity' survival at stake, it can and should be the case. And once again, this is where psychosocial and systems dynamics come in. Making sense and successfully managing forthcoming crises that have an increasingly greater potential to drastically alter the way life is organized requires countries to recognize they function as social systems; in particular why and how social defenses are mobilized against anxieties.

Forthcoming crises, those that humanity will wish nameless, are likely to be overwhelming. They are the type of issues that humanity must prepare for by reflecting collectively and, without any hindrance, psychosocially. As such, what follows provides examples of psychosocial issues that should be relevant to what could be some of the most salient crises in humanity's future.

Upon winning the 2021 Templeton Prize, Jane Goodall, the well-known primatologist, commented how humanity had basically brought the pandemic on itself because "our disrespect of the natural world was forcing animals closer to people and, as such, making it easier for pathogens to jump from an animal to a person." This well–established line of thinking, which also explains why collective needs to atone were identified earlier as initial psychosocial responses to the various lockdowns worldwide, provides the reason why protecting biodiversity is essential to preventing future pandemics. As such, in our quest to reflect psychosocially about the pandemic's aftermath, we begin by focusing on extinction threats.

We start with what should be high on the list of humanity's pressing concerns, something whose mental representation should be a source of such anxieties that it should foremost be on our mind. And that is the Anthropocene extinction of species. But yet, this nevertheless seems to be experienced as if dormant in our collective conscience. While there have already been five mass extinctions whereas a large share of earth's life forms quickly disappeared, the sixth one, which is ongoing, uniquely stands out as it is for the very first time the direct result of mankind's activity. As such, unless enough is done to prevent its totality, it will be our collective and undoubtedly most enduring legacy. And it is happening right now, for all of us to witness.

As eloquently stated in the extinction rebellion website, "We are on the brink of a global catastrophe. Life on Earth is in danger, with scientists agreeing we are entering a period of climate and ecological breakdown. From wildfires to heat waves, droughts to rising sea levels, the symptoms of our inaction will only worsen, the longer we take to address the causes of the crisis."[2] As David Grann indicated in his review of Kolbert's "The sixth Extinction," stories about extinction often read "like a scientific thriller-only more terrifying because it is real." See, Kolbert (2014). This sheer terror, a source of unfathomable anxieties, is precisely also the reason why Greta Thunberg, the young Swedish environmental activist who rose to fame following her school strike for climate solo demonstration in front of the Swedish parliament in Stockholm, has been denigrated with so much intensity. The greater the anxiety, the harsher and, often more perverse, the response of shooting the messenger will be. In a desperate wish not to confront undeniable truths, those opposing her message exploited her autism diagnosis to destroy her credibility. Happily, in a powerful move, Greta Thunberg used her own diagnosis to empower herself and, as a result, boost her credibility even further.

As Susan Long argued in a seminal article on ecological breakdown, denial can become so pervasive that it becomes a systemic process that ends up shaping an entire culture. See, Long (2015). It is precisely at that juncture that denial can become unusually harmful. Denial will be particularly strong whenever a system of beliefs becomes part of the group's identity, or social makeup. With the loss of identity often experienced by the group as its own psychological death, successfully mobilizing a denial social defense becomes essential to the group's survival when they are unable to mobilize a transformation. As a consequence, contrary to what rationality would suggest, when confronted by scientific evidence contradicting its core beliefs, group members often respond by doubling down rather than weakening or abandoning its own denial. This was, for example, observed in Australia where the government denied that the devastating bush fires of the Southern hemisphere summer of 2020 were caused by climate change. Unsurprisingly, this has not been specific to Australia. This type of denial, on the increase since the pandemic, has also figured prominently in the United States where assertions of environmental breakdown were also experienced by some as an attack on identity.

This psychosocial mechanism is fundamental to understand and take into account. It is at the very core of why myriads of well-meaning intents at winning over "others" to one's cause end up deepening rather than weakening splitting. Regardless of the evidence that is presented, no matter how overwhelmingly convincing it might appear to be, attempts at crossing ideological divides often fail. Listening to "others," simply experiencing for oneself the psychosocial world of these "others," can go a long way into setting the stage for being heard. Communication deprived of the generosity and humbleness that comes with such willingness is almost always bound to fail.

The pandemic, a psychosocial shock to most in light of the anxieties caused by both the existence of a deadly yet unseen pathogen and highly restrictive measures never experienced before, became in our view the perfect vehicle to express anxieties related to climate change. As argued earlier, restrictive measures to control the pandemic and even vaccines were often experienced as attempts by overarching governments to further extend their control over their constituents. While this was likely the result of a displacement, the true source of anxieties being the pandemic itself, this psychosocial response has also been observed in response to policies surrounding environmental breakdown. As such, climate change is becoming a new front in the identity wars. Resistance to "climate lockdown" (a term used by climate sceptics to denounce government-imposed restrictions they fear may be imposed in the name of climate change), the rallying cry to oppose the perceived conspiracy by global powers to increasingly restrict individual freedoms, has found a voice. Thus, the anguish and frustration of the pandemic has not only allowed public health but also environmental issues to become an integral part of identity politics. As a consequence, pandemic related public policy health responses and environmental concerns joined migration, which until now had been the sole and most prominent policy issue acting as a marker of identity.

Similar concerns have been expressed with health passes (e.g., *pass sanitaire* in France used to check vaccination status or exposure to the virus). The issue is somewhat different though as one of the underlying anxieties was due to fears of unrestricted authoritarianism in an age where technology allows for Orwellian type government controls that were simply unthinkable not that long ago. Thus in France, the country of the *Gilets Jaunes* movement, the continued appearance of new variants, decreased vaccination effectiveness, and the fact that most activities (even going to a coffee shop) were infringed upon by public health regulations gave rise to strong feelings that the government was taking advantage of the public health situation to increase the scope of its controls. These feelings also existed among vaccinated individuals who were among those voicing opposition to the health passes. Furthermore, the sharp differences in views surrounding risk assessment and management of the pandemic between those that chose to be vaccinated and the minority that did not allowed for a deflection of the blame away from governments towards the minority. The increased splitting, with the original bad object substituted for a new one, facilitated governments' implementation of drastic controls. As always, these policy measures would have benefitted from ex-ante psychosocial understanding of the issues.

While the psychosocial dynamics described above might seem intractable, this is not necessarily the case. While it might be too late to embark on a psychosocial based dialogue once denial social defenses are actually mobilized, nothing precludes preemptive and ongoing dialogue about the underlying psychosocial dynamics (e.g., overwhelming fear, disappearance of trust) as well as about the anxieties that underpin the social defenses mobilized by the group.

But for now, the pandemic, as a consequence of widely and intensely felt anxieties that could not be ignored, appears to have increased the propensity for so-called fringe or radical groups to adopt rhetoric that the majority of the population still experiences as extreme and even dangerous. With this unleashed, what was experienced and reacted to psychosocially with Covid-19 and its accompanying array of restrictive measures was also transposed to climate change. Both Covid-19 and climate change—as well as any proposed mitigating measures to deal with them—became markers of identity. With societies already divided along cultural markers of identity, splitting quickly intensified. Psychosocial storms that were already brewing quickly erupted. But rather than automatically take at face value what some groups indicate, no matter how extreme some of their positions are perceived to be, it would instead be paramount to systematically, albeit cautiously, interpret and understand what genuinely is being said.

This was, for example, mentioned earlier regarding vaccines. In a counterintuitive fashion, the debate turned out to be often stifled by those in favor of massive vaccination campaigns. Maybe their keen appreciation of the high cost, if not impossibility, of reaching herd immunity through infection rather than vaccination made them wary of setting up a safe space to discuss alternatives. Yet, it backfired. Incidentally, it also led to "only in America" grotesque albeit shameful (given the lack of vaccines in the developing world) policies of states like Ohio putting aside lotteries with winnings of one million dollars to convince recalcitrant vaccine takers. Instead, as is the norm in psychosocial dialogue, it would have been highly preferable to discuss all issues surrounding vaccines, while suspending all prior judgments, in a safe and inclusive space where issues such as fears surrounding their long-term effects might have been genuinely freely expressed. The same approach would also have been applicable to the mitigating measures, especially the lockdowns. It will also be relevant in the future to collective efforts to address climate change.

To explore this further, we now turn to QAnon, an example of those so-called conspiracy theory groups, which also espoused its own narratives regarding the pandemic. These groups are becoming increasingly relevant. In fact, Covid-19 allowed groups such as QAnon to expand, notably by incorporating in their message conspiracy theories about the pandemic. QAnon was well placed to incorporate anti-vaccine sentiments into its message since these fits perfectly a core belief that authority should never be trusted. It also provided the perfect entry point for QAnon to expand in Europe, notably in France and Germany, by focusing on the idea that the pandemic is part of a plan imposed by world elites to dominate, through imposed vaccination, most of the world's population. Seeing themselves as victims of a threatening and dangerous State, demonstrators in the United States, the UK and last but not least, Germany, compared themselves to Jews in Nazi Germany by wearing a yellow star with "Jude" replaced by "ungeimpft," or unvaccinated. The comparison, while unsettling to say the least, is also a way to diminish the seriousness of the Holocaust by trivializing it, in part through provocation. As its conspiracy theory also deepened, QAnon even argued that the goal was to inject every individual with a GPS microchip as a way to track everyone; a reference to the perception of Orwellian controls. And last, statements comparing Covid-19 vaccines to weapons of mass destruction designed to wipe out the human race highlight how extinction anxieties reawakened by the pandemic became verbalized, in displacement, through the mistrust of vaccines. Similar behaviors are also likely to be mobilized by such groups if and when other systemic crises hit.

At heart is a message that empowers followers to annihilate "in the mind" elites that are experienced as controlling the world and, equally importantly, depreciating them. The message should probably not be taken as face value. Instead, what matters is the social defense, that the message induces followers to mobilize. In both cases, while expressed drastically differently, the message is about shielding oneself from perverse individuals (the elites) determined to controlling the world. While only a hypothesis here, I would suspect that a large share of QAnon supporters might not even believe to the letter the message of pervert (more specifically pedophile as QAnon supporters often express it) elites. What matters is their conviction that these elites are bent on exploiting the world to their benefit no matter the consequences. They are, therefore, expressing a disgust, as well as resentment and envy, of elites that are systematically able to get away with abusing the system to their own benefit. In displacement, the mental representation of that abuse becomes that of a pedophile sexually abusing a defenseless—and pure—child. And yet, supreme irony, one of the individuals that participated in the January 6 attack on the Capitol and shouted, "You guys like protecting pedophiles?" had himself been convicted of unlawful sex with a minor.

In a strange twist, while Trump seemingly met all the criteria to be associated with those elites (in a way no different than what the Clintons may have represented), he nevertheless was able to connect with supporters, some of whom undoubtedly identified with QAnon, because he enabled them to identify with him. As such, Trump—talking directly to them and like them—was able to have his constituents perceive him as one of them. They not only felt heard but more importantly felt that he spoke on their behalf by being the maverick that would destroy the system that was overwhelming them.

WHAT IS BEING SAID AND WHAT IS BEING HEARD

The above example highlights the importance of hearing what is behind what is being said by each group as opposed to automatically eschewing communication with another group because of splitting social defenses. Regarding splitting, one must differentiate situations whereas groups become incapable of hearing one another, what I would consider genuine splitting, from those whereas groups choose in retaliation or contempt to deliberately ignore one another. Regardless, both forms can potentially be confronted by creating a space in which genuine communication and understanding is allowed to take place, both between and within groups. This is important: what is heard is not necessarily what is meant. And what is said may not reflect the underlying cause of the emotion felt. I suspect that this may be true with QAnon. Again, rather than genuinely believing in the existence of Satanists pedophile elites preying on children, adherents and sympathizers are more likely using these mental representations to express their disgust, contempt, and rejection of the perceived perverse societal dynamics. Incidentally (and scarily), these fantasies are not that far removed from Middle Age fantasies of Jews stealing and murdering Christian children to use their blood to make Matzah.

Another illustration of the importance of correctly hearing is the following. In working with radicalized youth in Tunisia, including individuals that ultimately left for Syria to join the ranks of the Islamist State (Daesh), Ben Smaïl and Boccara (2015) showed that joining Daesh was almost always in response to a rebellion against a world that had become futureless and meaningless. In fact, contrary to what most would expect, religion had little to do with joining an Islamist movement. At the peak of foreigners joining the organization, local commanders were baffled at the complete lack of knowledge of—or interest in—Islam amongst some of the youth that had travelled all the way to Syria to join Daesh's ranks.

Thus, it was found that the wish to repair a damaged identity by being accepted into a uniquely strong community of *frères* (brothers) and the protection offered against the intrusion of alternative subjectivities, especially the feminine, in the public space were the key determinants of joining Daesh. This explains why many European recruits did not even come from Muslim backgrounds while recruits from Tunisia were often not from very religious families. Incidentally, Daesh's jihadist videos, a lot of them in languages other than Arabic, were less prone to mention God and focused instead on perverse societal dynamics, for example in reference to injustice or unfairness, which often figured prominently in their message. As such, Daesh not only transcended cultures but also religions.

Therefore, central to the existence of groups such as QAnon or even Daesh are the perceived existence of perverse societal dynamics. For example, there was ample evidence during the pandemic that social media companies allowed their own algorithms to amplify and manipulate information without much regard for the validity of the content that was being disseminated. Focusing solely on profits, regardless of the nature of the psychosocial dynamics that were encouraged, social media companies failed to monitor contents as long as those encouraged users to engage, hence provided additional revenues.

To these dynamics we now turn.

PSYCHOSOCIAL EXTINCTION

We begin with an overview of the perverse societal dynamics, as opposed to the social defenses on which we focused earlier, that provided the backdrop to the pandemic and are, as such, likely to figure prominently when and if another systemic crisis hits.

At the time the pandemic struck, societal anxieties, thanks to rapid disruptions to ways of lives brought about by globalization, were likely to have already been high and largely shared. How various nations faced the pandemic was essentially driven by the nature of their societal level object relations. The latter are first and foremost determined by the extent to which perverse societal dynamics, buttressed by narcissism and instrumental relations, have taken hold.

Note the deliberate choice of using the term "object relations." In psychoanalysis, the latter refers to the ways relationships between individuals are formed and influenced by these individuals' internal images. Regarding the latter, the infant's relationship to the mother, the first external object, is a strong determinant of the formation of personality. Extending the concept, a society, like a mother, also plays a containing role. The quality of inter-personal relationships has a significant influence on whether a society is able to function as a good container. Inter-personal relationships in a society are strongly influenced by the latter's imprint on individuals; in other words by the mental representations, country romance, shared identity, and even the nature of the social defenses. For example, in France, societal object relations are relatively often beset by aggression. Yet, unlike in the US, it is almost always verbalized rather than enacted. Furthermore, the society there is often more capable than others to coalesce around social solidarity ideas and shared objectives.

Our hypothesis is that the worldwide malaise that the pandemic ultimately brought to the forefront can be interpreted as a response to the despair and anxieties brought by social systems experienced as perverse and unfair. Furthermore the perverse societal dynamics that underpin those feelings are more often than not, as was the case with social media influential postings and conspiracy theories surrounding the pandemic, the result of many actors colluding with one another. Fundamentally, the culture's obsession with individual pleasure, often at the expense of others, leads to a sense of deprivation and destroys meaning. As such, as already underscored in the previous section, some individuals perceive elites as denigrating them. The latter, as objects of contempt, are likely to experience their powerlessness as psychological death. The ensuing feeling of alienation and revulsion at the perverse system can become unbearable and, as such, leads to wishes to "exit" the system. This explains the renewed attractiveness of extremist organizations that are experienced as capable of repairing narcissism. The anxieties triggered by the pandemic favored extremism, which for some became a safe retreat. As such, splitting and violent enactments increased during the pandemic. This was, for example in evidence with increased anti-Semitism in the United States, Hindu nationalism in India, or increased domestic violence in France as well as in Malaysia, Lebanon and China and also in Australia, Cyprus, and Argentina.

In this chapter, we began with the pandemic's origin, which in Jane Goodall's words was the outcome of our collective disrespect of the environment. This led us to link the pandemic to the sixth—or Anthropocene—extinction; the first endogenous extinction since it is exclusively driven by human impact on the planet. This, in turn, took us to the heart of what made the pandemic such a formidable event. It not only had the capacity to provoke anxieties on a globalized scale rarely seen before but also increased humanity's awareness of psychosocial dynamics that it had, until then, mostly turned a blind eye to. While existing social defenses made it possible to deny threats to our environment, the specificity of the pandemic and of its aftermath is that it may no longer be possible to maintain such a denial.

As a consequence, in line with our increased collective internalization of the extreme risks posed by the ongoing environmental degradation, I believe that it has now become relevant to talk about the equally extreme risks of what I would like to call a psychosocial extinction.

Once again, our line of reasoning remains exclusively from a systems dynamics perspective. For example, arguing that a society is failing to be "empathetic enough" does not imply that its members may lack empathic capability at the individual level. Our interest lies at the level of the entire group, in other words whether members of the society are capable of having empathy for individuals with whom they do not necessarily have a personal interaction. Our emphasis throughout is on a society's capacity to contain its members. The latter would be reflected in its psychosocial resilience, meaning the resilience of the social system to confront psychosocial crises. Furthermore, a society's capacity for empathy and psychosocial resilience is not static. For example, a society confronting psychosocial shocks such a public health emergency, devastating environmental degradation or internal tensions is more likely to see that capacity decrease. Unless it has the ability as a social system to work through these issues, it will likely remain unable to successfully address those psychosocial shocks. It is precisely the capacity to collectively work through psychosocial issues that makes a society resilient in the face of psychosocial crises.

By psychosocial extinction, we are referring to an increasingly large share of countries worldwide losing the capacity to work through and, as such, losing empathic capability as well as psychosocial resilience. Several Western countries are witnessing a decrease in that capability; in part because of the speed and superficiality of social media interactions. In such a society, individuals lose genuineness and aliveness. Authenticity is lost as a result of an increasing number of social interactions losing spontaneity, for example with everything "choreographed" to be "Instagram able." In many aspects, we are truly in a world characterized by experiences of "false self."[3] The concept, an outcome linked to a defense, can be extended to a large group. In fact, without using the terminology at the time, this is exactly the psychosocial environment that characterized Ben Ali's Tunisia; an unbearable burden that ultimately led to the Arab Spring. See, Boccara (2014).

In such a world, meaning is lost and societies break down.

Thus, as we saw earlier, a culture of narcissism, epidemic of indifference, and disappearing sense of relatedness led individuals, particularly in the United States, to face the pandemic together yet alone. It was also argued that in promoting individualism, consumerist societies had considerably weakened individuals' capacity to identify with one another. This, in turn, was exacerbated further by the Internet and social media, which paradoxically have brought individuals much closer together while at the same time profoundly isolating them from one another.

PREPARING FOR THE FUTURE

The pandemic made acutely stark the fact that a successful preparation for its aftermath will require collective psychosocial work on the issues identified in this book. Understanding social defenses and systems dynamics matter. With policy responses to the pandemic often "hijacked" by social defenses, institutions failed to protect people. Thus, as argued earlier, China was too slow in allowing the world to understand what was happening and precious time was lost. But, as was also argued, what transpired in China was also observed elsewhere as was the case with the delays and backtracking on policy measures observed in so many countries as well as with the WHO. Therefore, it is likely that the pandemic could have been substantially mitigated, if not altogether avoided.

In addition, it is also likely that precious opportunities were quickly lost in preventing Covid-19 to become endemic. Early calls on the importance to stop Covid-19, such as those issued by the well-known epidemiologist Dr. Eric Feigl-Ding were sadly dismissed,[4] including by some physicians, with the catastrophic consequences that we now know. The probability of immune-escaping variants taking hold is very high in a highly, yet incompletely, vaccinated population since the virus is able to adapt to the existing vaccines. Yet, a large share of the world was all too quick to let go of social distancing and mask wearing under the illusion that vaccination alone could end the pandemic. While there were ample warnings about the potentially significant long-term risks of being infected, even mildly, with Covid-19, those were largely ignored. Similarly, there was an extreme reluctance and, as a consequence, long delays accepting that Covid-19 was mainly spread through aerosols (fine particles that may stay suspended for hours) rather larger droplets that quickly fall to the ground and contaminate surfaces.

These tragic mistakes also led the UN Secretary General to talk about the dangers of "a two-speed global response" in facing "a situation in which rich countries vaccinate the majority of their people and open their economies, while the virus continues to cause deep suffering by circling and mutating in the poorest countries."[5] For the world as a whole to end-up acquiring herd immunity through exposure[6]—and death—rather than vaccination would be a catastrophic moral failure. This is a dangerous outcome. It will only reinforce nationalism and, as such, decrease global solidarity at a time when it is needed the most. While splitting between nations can be ill afforded during global crises, it seems increasingly likely that large swaths of humanity could be forced to fend for themselves in the aftermath of the pandemic. This would, for example, be the case following a major climate event affecting disproportionally poorer regions without any meaningful assistance from the rest of the world: already the psychosocial dynamics observed with migration today.

The paragraph above highlights how psychosocial dynamics between countries, in other words looking at the entire world as one social system, can play out similarly and even more intensely than what has already been identified within specific countries. As decried by the United Nations, empathic availability at the level of the entire world went missing. In fact, national borders' psychosocial function is to enable the mobilization of splitting social defenses with the least possible resistance. Thus, national borders validated splitting at a time that it was at its most destructive since a respiratory agent pandemic cannot be managed in isolation. And yet, forthcoming crises will increasingly require working psychosocially from the perspective of the entire world as a social system. As shown by most of the UN initiatives, this is not, however, necessarily what multilateralism can achieve Depending upon the incentives structure, nations cooperating with one another as independent social systems may (or may not, the most likely situation) yield a different outcome than nations working together as a single social system.

Unsurprisingly, the same behaviors are also in evidence with climate change as was starkly demonstrated during the 2021 United Nations Climate Change Conference (COP26). As stated earlier, Covid-19 denial is shifting to climate denial since the narratives concerning sinister plots to control populations are identical and driven by the same anxieties.

Sadly, a lot of the participants at the COP26, in particular youth activists from the most vulnerable regions, left disappointed with little hope that the agreements reached in Glasgow will be enough to save their communities from the devastating impact of climate change. Furthermore, several countries felt betrayed by the last-minute watering down of the original phasing out clause of coal power, the single most important source of greenhouse gas emissions. In fact, the COP26 President even apologized to the most vulnerable nations for how the summit ended and the UN Secretary General, deploring the inability of the summit to overcome deep contradictions, indicated that that the time had come to go into emergency mode. The tragic consequence though is that the world is now assumed to be on track for a 2.4 C temperature increase by the end of the century; a catastrophic level far in excess of the 1.5 C temperature increase that the world has always known should not breached. While COP26 nevertheless achieved what could have been significant progress by the standards of earlier climate conference, the achievements to date are too little too late. The climate crisis will only be solved if net zero emissions can be genuinely achieved. While some argue that the UN conference was not the catastrophe that many implied in the sense that it succeeded in completely changing the debate, COP26 coupled with the ongoing saga surrounding the pandemic are creating a perfect psychosocial storm. As such, humanity's future will depend on its readiness to make collective decisions to address forthcoming systemic crises, especially those related to the environmental breakdown.

However, contrary to what might have until recently been hoped for, what we have introduced as a psychosocial extinction is threatening humanity's ability to address forthcoming crises and is, as such, destabilizing the planet.

One of the psychosocial defining characteristics of our times has been the proliferation of fake news and of conspiracy theories. The fact that this occurred during a health crisis, an area where science and rationality driven cooperation should have been the norm, is particularly unsettling. Yet, it should not come as a surprise. The pandemic, and all the conspiracy theories that came with it, could only aggravate the already significant distrust of the State that was the hallmark of many groups. These groups, usually found at the right of the political spectrum, are not only often targeted by fake news but also have a greater tendency to believe the latter. This makes sense since believing in fake news is consistent with the mobilization of social defenses in response to their distrust of the State; a dangerous object that is not to be trusted. As such, fake news decrease anxieties (what is wished for can be heard) since it validates the distrust of the State. Merging "in the mind" the media with the State leads to a rejection of the former in the form of trusting alternative views. This is, in turn, experienced as an act of defiance towards the elites; listening to fake news becoming a way to enact one's aggression towards them.

And last, we also need to mention cyber warfare, one of the single most frightening threats that should be of concern in the aftermath of the pandemic. And if there are any doubts, attacks even occurred against public health agencies during the pandemic and research institutions working on vaccines. For example, in June 2017, Ukraine became victim of Russia unleashing "the most destructive and costly cyber-attack in world history. That afternoon Ukrainians woke up to black screens everywhere. They could not take money from ATM's, pay for gas at stations, send or receive mail, pay for a train ticket, buy groceries, get paid or—perhaps most terrifying of all—monitor radiation levels at Chernobyl." See, Perlroth (2021). What took place in Ukraine could happen anywhere. In fact, cyber-attacks have risen dramatically during the pandemic. Opportunities for cyber criminals to exploit vulnerabilities rapidly increased with businesses having to deploy systems and networks to enable employees to work from home. The United States was particularly vulnerable. As a spoiled society enamored with convenience, the US as a social system was all too eager to idealize the idea of being able to manage one's entire life remotely on the internet, albeit at the risk of destroying daily interactions and therefore the social fabric of the nation. Furthermore, the country having fallen behind nations such as Russia or China seems insufficiently prepared to thwart cyber-attacks that could wreak havoc on its population. In fact, the United States suffered 65,000 ransom ware attacks in 2020.[7] While the solutions can only be technical, it should also be helpful for private companies and the public sector to think psychosocially through the meaning of those attacks; in other words how they are experienced. This is particularly relevant psychosocially because the latter are often experienced as an attack on a company's integrity and as a loss of omnipotence. This must have been the case with the May 2021 cyber-attack against the Colonia pipeline in the United States that led the to the shutdown of its entire operation.[8] While the Justice department was able to trace and recover much of the ransom payment, this is unlikely to become the norm. The potential level of anxieties is such that cybercrime warrants—as would have been the case with terrorism prior to September 11—supportive psychosocial interventions. Doing so would avoid taking the risk of policy responses to cybercrime being potentially hijacked by social defenses. Lack of or delays in preparedness often have a psychosocial, rather than solely, a technical dimension.

We now turn to Estonia, a country where psychosocial issues often take center stage. The Estonia example below clearly shows how psychosocial preparedness has the potential to positively impact outcomes. As Volkan (1997) showed with his psychosocial interventions in the Baltic nation, groups that feel psychosocially separated from one another but yet share the same space (in this case, ethnic Estonians and ethnic Russians in Estonia) need to maintain a psychological border between them; recognizing differences a way to protect each group's unique identity. As such, the removal of a Soviet WWII memorial in Tallinn in 2007 led not only to violent clashes within the country but also to Estonia itself becoming the target of what at the time was the biggest cyber-attack against a single country. Yet, fortunately for Estonia, the nation had already had the unique opportunity to explore over a period of several years these large group identity issues. The Carter center sponsored interventions that included a team of psychoanalysts, including Vamik Volkan, who all understood the specific issues surrounding large group identity. As such, years later, the government was immediately able to realize that safeguarding a healthy internal psychosocial environment meant that preparedness for cyber-attacks had to be treated the same way the nation protected itself from military invasions. Having internalized psychosocially what their wish for independence from the former Soviet Union while maintaining harmony between Russian and non-Russian residents of the country genuinely involved, the country quickly built itself as the world's leader in cyber security strategy. It digitized earlier than most countries, invested heavily in digitalization awareness campaigns, especially for senior citizens, and emphasized coding in its schools' curricula. As a consequence, Estonia, which has all of its data backed up in a secure center in Luxembourg, was chosen as the home of NATO's cyber defense hub.

Another issue of concern for the aftermath is how governments that suddenly found themselves with unprecedented powers experienced it and whether they may be tempted to keep it. While France established extensive arrays of controls, special signed authorization needed to leave's one house and fines for non-compliance strictly enforced, it also reinforced other restrictions during that the pandemic, notably on immigration and security. In Hungary, the government passed legislation to authorize it to rule by decree. Thus, a key issue will be whether and how governments will scale back. And this is psychosocially also relevant to fiscal and monetary policies whereas authorities adopted extraordinary emergency measures that would have been unthinkable before the pandemic. As always, public policy measures such as these also have psychosocial components. As such, it would also be important for both fiscal and authorities to reflect psychosocially on ways in which these times were experienced.

The unending and increasing anxieties bode poorly for the future. In November 2021, several European governments reintroduced drastic restrictions on their citizens due to sudden sharp increases in the number of new contaminations. In doing so without adequate psychosocial support and messaging, European governments often ended-up reinforcing, rather than decreasing in intensity, the mobilization of the social defenses that have been repeatedly identified in the book. While the vaccines are thought to be effective against serious forms of the disease, they effectiveness at limiting contamination is now known to be poor. This has made it harder to sustain magical thinking surrounding the vaccines. Experienced as a betrayal, the inability to continue successfully mobilizing an undoing social defense has led to a disavowal of the system, which is embodied by both the State and the big pharmaceutical companies. This explains the sudden and often violent response against rigid health passes and mandatory vaccination. The automatic exclusion of unvaccinated individuals from public life is promoting the mobilization of regressed splitting social defenses as well as demonization of those individuals. With the short effectiveness of the vaccines, whose long-term risks are not fully known, transmission risks increase quickly unless vaccinated individuals receive booster regularly. This is unlikely to be sustainable.

Going back to government's monitoring of its own citizens, there needs to be a reflection on how authorities reacted/experienced both the special legislative framework and the challenges they faced; for example anti-lockdowns protests and difficulties in crafting public health policy messages. And citizens groups would also need to do the same. For example, regarding the latter the restrictions imposed may have acted as a container, reassuring citizens, or, on the contrary may have reinforced mental representations of an elitist State infantilizing, if not even denigrating, its own citizens. Of course, both could hold; each mental representation being that of a specific group at a specific time within the society.

It is also important to take into consideration that the pandemic occurred at a time when surveillance technology is evolving very fast; governments now able to monitor citizens in ways that were absolutely unthinkable to authoritarian regimes in previous generations. To make things worse, the Internet renders citizens willing, even eager, to share all of their data, thus providing a detailed picture of their lives. Big Data algorithms can predict collective behaviors that individuals may not even be aware of and, as such, intervene in psychosocial processes in Orwellian ways that, until now, resided only in our collective imagination. This is something that has major implications as it could herald the end of freedom. See, Han (2017).

As emphasized by Harari (2020), "if corporations and governments start harvesting our biometric data en masse, they can get to know us far better than we know ourselves, and they can then not just predict our feelings but also manipulate our feelings and sell us anything they want—be it a product or a politician." The almost apocalyptic vision of what that warning entails makes a strong case for collective and inclusive efforts in societies to truly explore the meaning of everything that transpired during the pandemic.

As mentioned earlier in the case of South Korea' successful approach to managing the pandemic, contact tracing, which required stringent monitoring, did not involve coercive measures because trust in the government and the information it provides ran high. Citizens did not have to be disempowered. This provides another justification for promoting psychosocial interventions aimed at restoring meaning through the internalization of the way a society functions as a social system. Societies that effectively contain their members have a greater propensity to allow trust to develop between members of the societies and between members of the societies and their institutions. One can think of this as basic trust at the societal level.[9] This is also the case in Japan, a country that had momentarily fallen behind but was able to successfully alter the course of the pandemic.

To conclude, the pandemic has brought to the forefront that humanity is facing extraordinary challenges on a scale rarely seen before. Besides the ecological threats, there exists an information breakdown and economic structural changes that are creating an ultra-rich class (proliferation of billionaires) and an army of destitute trapped in countries vulnerable to climate change and future pandemics. The seriousness of what is transpiring all around us is something that is increasingly being internalized as calls to change course are not only becoming more frequent but also come from increasingly widely trusted sources.[10] Yet the window of opportunity to act is shrinking. Short of a robust internalization of the psychosocial dynamics surrounding these challenges, the probability of irreversible changes to our environment will only increase, resulting in humanity taking colossal risks with its future.

As anxieties become nearly insurmountable nearly everywhere, windows of opportunities to successfully undo the psychosocial extinction threatening humanity's future may fast disappear. Now is the time for a psychosocial renewal.

PSYCHOSOCIAL RENEWAL: THE AUDACITY OF A REPAIR ACT

Neoliberal consumerist societies promote narcissism and, as such, a world devoid of individuals genuinely willing to care for one another. This is because our self worth becomes based upon what we own (or experience) in comparison to others and, as such, in our capacity to trigger envy. Consumerism induces individuals to display, often through social media, an often-illusionary *Jouissance*. See, Lacan (1972–73). Fighting the frustration created by a system that produces envy, individuals feel the need to highlight ways in which their life is better than that of other's. The system promotes this kind of behavior by seeing individuals solely as consumers. These behaviors increase what has increasingly become an otherwise depreciated self-worth. The latter is a key outcome of consumerist societies, for whom an addiction to *Jouissance* becomes essential to their survival.

As such, narcissistic entitlement is probably today's Achilles' heel gripping our world. Promoting narcissistic withdrawal as a way to overcome this is in our view the most pressing challenge facing humanity today.

While narcissistic withdrawal (at the societal level) is first and foremost a psychosocial issue, its counterpart, narcissistic entitlement, cannot be understood without reference to economics. As mentioned throughout the book, psychosocial dynamics play out simultaneously at the unconscious and the conscious level, or "below" and "above" the surface. As such, successfully modifying psychosocial dynamics requires working both "below" and "above" the surface, in other words at both the psychosocial/systems dynamics level and the incentive structure level. This is what makes Socio Analytic Dialogue thinking relevant since it builds on both psychoanalysis (adapted to large groups) and on an economics/political science. Narcissism entitlement and its corresponding addiction to *Jouissance* would be much harder to sustain in an economic structure that would no longer emphasize that pleasure can almost only be derived from the acquisition and consumption of goods.

As argued by Long (2008) in a different context, the aspects of perverse societal dynamics that are relevant to understanding the pandemic and its aftermath are as follows. First and foremost is the predominance of instrumental relations, whereas most interactions are motivated by narcissistic gratification. This leads to individuals experiencing pleasure at the expense of others. The latter become "in the mind" objects to be used and whose existence, as such, is not fully recognized. The above is at the foundation of the perverse societal dynamics that underpin so many of the behaviors that are discussed throughout this book. As seen earlier, it is precisely because the solidarity and collective efforts required in confronting the pandemic deprived individuals of narcissistic gratification that efforts failed in most consumerist societies whose social compact was weak. In addition, to be sustained, any perverse societal dynamics need to be denied. But yet, reality, whether it is the pandemic, the impending environmental catastrophe, or the rising and likely unsustainable income inequalities is often acknowledged. However, this is a defense. It allows the perverse system to avoid blame. By claiming its awareness of the consequences of perversion and in its denial of it being the culprit, it fails to do anything about any perversion in response. As Long (2008) argues, "the system both knows and does not know." And last, in a defensive attempt to validate the psychosocial environment that is wished for, the perverse societal dynamics are sustained by the engagement of accomplices (conscious or unconscious collusions), whose relationships to one another insures loyalty to the group and, if relevant, to its leader.

This makes for a quite a resilient psychosocial environment that, at least on the surface, may appear to be extraordinarily difficult to change. While undoubtedly true, the reminder of the book focuses on finding, or restoring, meaning through psychosocial dialogue as a way to move societies away from these perverse dynamics. Doing so requires neutrality akin to what is referred to as psychoanalytic neutrality, albeit again adapted to large groups for our purpose. The psychosocial approach that is proposed is based on the exploration, each group freely sharing its own mental representations and anxieties, of the society as a social system without setting any specific goals. What we are suggesting can be thought of as a shared psychosocial journey exploring various aspects of the society's splitting divides. The deliberate absence of a specific purpose is precisely what may promote (positive) identification and, as a consequence, empathic availability at the societal level. One can think of the approach as a mutual exploration with groups in the society trading with one another their psychosocial experiences, the latter experienced by each recipient group as if it was its own. The "as if" is the prelude to the otherwise often elusive identification between groups.

An important aspect of the dialogue that is suggested as a way to being able to navigate existing societal splits (as opposed to remaining solely on one side of the splitting divides) is its neutrality. One could say that it is apolitical. Yet this would be missing an important point. It is apolitical but only in the sense that, by working at a societal unconscious level, it works at a level where convergence of affects, rather than divergence of the latter, becomes more of the norm. This is because groups that belong to the same social system often share the same anxieties. For example, two groups split from one another may both experience non-verbalized anxieties due to each experiencing their identity to be threatened. But if, in time, each group can verbalize and communicate the latter, this is likely to allow the groups to recognize the commonalities of their anxieties and, more generally, of their psychosocial experiences. As the consequence, each group reaches a position where it becomes capable of humanizing the other. Verbalization can be a powerful tool towards allowing each group to appreciate one another's affects and become more aware of their commonalities rather than their differences.

To illustrate how apolitical the thinking should be considered in spite of issues that are often splitting groups violently from one another, let me illustrate what I describe above with the United States as a social system. The United States, which has had a considerable influence on many nations adopting several aspects of the so-called American way of life, is used here as an example and the same could be written—even if some of the psychosocial issues may differ—for many other nations.

Overall, and the more so before the country began its vaccination drive, the argument in the book has been critical of the United States' handling of the pandemic. However, the views were always expressed from the perspective of the country as a social system. As such, there was no implicit "indicting" of either the authorities or the people on policy choice, policy implementation, or even behavioral responses to the latter. The "indictment" instead was that of the social system as a whole, in other words of the ways in which mental representations, psychosocial antecedents, anxieties, and social defenses mobilized against those anxieties all taken together led to situations that were not conducive to managing adequately the pandemic. In adopting such a perspective, blame becomes so diffused that it becomes shared by all. In other words, what makes a psychosocial and systems dynamics approach to public policy apolitical is that it takes place at the level of the entire social system. In doing so, it absconds from judging any group's behavior since, by default, what transpires in any society can only be seen as the result of the interplay of all the psychosocial dynamics. These include the unconscious collusions between groups, which define the social system at any given time.

From a psychosocial and systems dynamics perspective, we are always "all in this together." As a consequence, moving forward can only involve the entire society together. This built-in robust inclusiveness through a shared responsibility ethos is not only what sets the proposed approach apart from anything else but also what makes it the most—if not the only—adapted perspective to our dangerously split times.

As argued in Boccara (2014), psychoanalysis, applied and adapted to countries and public policies, allows for a uniquely profound and unparalleled understanding of the human psyche and psychosocial dynamics from a systems perspective because it focuses on unconscious motives and behaviors. Disagreements on public policies often provide a fertile ground for societal unconscious dynamics; particularly because policies can themselves become social defenses. This was clearly in evidence during the pandemic. As such, an in-depth understanding of the psychosocial dynamics underpinning each social system is essential to enable a society to manage what are increasingly becoming nearly insurmountable anxieties. The quality of the relationship to "others," or object relations at the level of the entire society, is absolutely essential in determining that society's capacity to work through the underlying psychosocial issues.

To these issues, we turn in chapters 6 and 7.

NOTES

1. "The war that could have been prevented," *Jerusalem Post*, May 6, 2015, https://www.jpost.com/opinion/the-war-that-could-have-been-prevented-402317.
2. https://rebellion.global/, accessed May 31, 2021.
3. The concept was introduced by D. Winnicott; a psychoanalyst of the British Object Relations school. In early development, the absence of "good enough" mothering induces a child to behave, really seduce, the mother (or mother substitute) by introjecting the behaviors that are perceived to be those that will lead to being contained. The false self, therefore, becomes the personality that is, "in the mind of the infant," expected from the mother. Genuineness and spontaneity die and are replaced by emptiness. It is a defense, which conceptually can easily be extended to a larger group.
4. "Why Was It So Hard to Raise the Alarm Bell on the Coronavirus?," *Intelligencer*, March 26, 2020, www.nymag.com/intelligencer/amp/2020/03/why-was-it-so-hard-to-raise-the-alarm-on-coronavirus.html.
5. "UN chief says world at 'war' against COVID-19," *Al-Jazeera*, May 24, 2020, https://www.aljazeera.com/news/2021/5/24/un-chief-says-world-at-war-against-covid-19.
6. In any case, it seems increasingly unlikely that exposure to Covid-19 is capable of providing lasting immunity, particularly as new variants keep emerging.
7. "U.S. Suffers Over 7 Ransom Ware Attacks an Hour. It's Now A National Security Risk," *NPR*, https://www.npr.org/2021/06/09/1004684788/u-s-suffers-over-7-ransomware-attacks-an-hour-its-now-a-national-security-risk.
8. "Hackers Breached Colonial Pipeline Using Compromised Password," *Bloomberg*, June 4, 2021, https://www.bloomberg.com/news/articles/2021-06-04/hackers-breached-colonial-pipeline-using-compromised-password.
9. Basic trust is used in psychoanalysis to describe how an infant benefitting from good mothering (a "good enough" container of anxieties) will develop the capacity to build trust in others, as he/she grows older. The State has an important containing function and can, as such, promote that capacity at the societal level, which is how basic trust is used here.
10. "Our Planet, Our Future: An Urgent Call for Action," *The National Academies of Sciences Engineering Medicine*, April 29, 2021, https://www.nationalacademies.org/news/2021/04/nobel-prize-laureates-and-other-experts-issue-urgent-call-for-action-after-our-planet-our-future-summit.

Chapter 6

Socio-Analytic Dialogue to the Rescue

INTRODUCING SOCIO-ANALYTIC DIALOGUE

It is still too early to know if, how, and to what extent the world will change as the result of the Covid-19 pandemic. But it increasingly looks like endemicity will prevail: several governments having already abandoned their containment strategies in favor of living with the virus. While some view the crisis unleashed by the pandemic as an opportunity to profoundly modify our relationship to the environment, in large part by significantly altering our economic system, the wish to go back to the world that once is undoubtedly very strong. To many, acting on this wish by undoing all that took place, appears to be the only way to successfully defend against the anxieties that were unleashed by the pandemic; witness, for example, the often-premature re-openings and the ways most behave once restrictions are lifted.

Nevertheless, the toll that endemicity will likely exert on societies is such that the pandemic will almost certainly induce significant changes in the ways our societies are organized. Denial of environmental and future pandemic risks has become harder to sustain. Furthermore, the capacity for collective denial is likely to be further weakened once government assistance, that was deployed as if fiscal constraints did not exist, dries out. The economic fallout (e.g., businesses permanent closures) and the debt constraints will not be easy to manage. To be successful, forthcoming attempts at thinking through and creating the post pandemic world will require societies and governments to successfully manage the underlying, and undoubtedly very complex, psychosocial environment. This section argues that this can only be achieved through and in-depth appreciation of underlying anxieties and affects and the promotion of empathic availability. Not doing so or not being able to do so will likely lead to the mobilization of increasingly regressed social defenses and a further weakening of existing social compacts. There would also be a greater propensity for public policies, increasingly "hijacked" as social defenses, to fail to successfully meet their objectives. This is, until now, what has already taken place in several countries, notably with increased splitting and collusive denial.

The pandemic, through widespread lockdowns, their economic consequences, and the closing down of national borders worldwide, has challenged like never before pervasive neoliberal thinking and its promotion of both unfettered economic growth and unchecked individualism. While it had been possible in the past only to sporadically focus on issues such as climate change or deepening economic inequalities, this is likely no longer the case. By exposing weaknesses, the pandemic can no longer allow a denial of responsibilities. See, Long (2015). Were denials to continue, humanity would likely soon reach unsustainable situations; something that cannot be excluded with endemicity and the continued emergence of new variants. Regardless, repeated, and at times subtle, forms of denials cannot be excluded. They, however, can only prolong for a relatively short time a status quo that is simply increasingly harder to sustain. In the words of Rosa (2020), "it is as if gigantic brakes had been applied to the accelerating society." While we have found ourselves powerless in the face of climate change, a psychosocial barrier may have been broken in finding ourselves capable of collectively controlling our actions in the world. The psychosocial shock turned out to be profound. Unlike responses to climate change, which can to some extent be put off, this crisis encompassed the entire world in only a few weeks. The unprecedented self-imposed economic depression, humanity collectively putting the brakes on all economic activities, may possibly lead humanity to reexamine existing economic arrangements and their relationship to the environment.

There are already many proposals on the table such as universal basic income (which Spain passed in May 2020), wealth taxes, and budgetary rules for social and environmental values. Thus, the tide could be turning away from laissez faire economics towards government activism, especially concerning public investment. In fact, some of those ideas have even been espoused in the Financial Times,[1] a publication otherwise known for its unequivocal embrace of neoliberalism. Ideas like those of Thomas Piketty, the well-known French economist who inspired the Occupy Wall Street movement, once considered far left, are now becoming mainstream. Last, the State that had traditionally been perceived as an obstacle to laissez faire economics and growth is now increasingly seen as the entity most capable of spearheading innovation, as was the case with research on vaccines undertaken in publicly funded laboratories. In fact, companies like Apple. Google, and Tesla benefitted greatly from state investment at their onset.

Yet, what all of this suggests is that anxieties were so high, even if left unspoken during lockdowns, that governments found themselves willing to violate what had otherwise always been considered sacrosanct economic constraints. As such, and for different reasons, anxieties—when the bill comes due—are also likely to be high during the pandemic's aftermath. As a consequence, while endless economic growth may now be seen as the villain, with globalization and environmental degradation spearheading the emergence and diffusion of new diseases, many could still nevertheless reject the idea that greed driven profit maximization is the culprit behind preventing mankind from existing in balance with the environment.

Therefore, in light of the complexities and uncertainties still surrounding the pandemic and its aftermath, it is probably best to promote psychosocial environments that tolerate ambivalence and uncertainty. This is not the case right now as illustrated from a psychoanalytic perspective with Johanssen (2021), who writes from a Kleinian perspective, arguing that we are finding ourselves in a regressed Paranoid-Schizoid position rather than the more adaptive Depressive position. The world, which is currently going through grief on a planetary scale, is split. Therefore, it needs to find ways to move away from the current defensive position it is in so as to allow a healthier and more inclusive debate on what's ahead. At a time when, at least for now, humanity's omnipotence has been shattered, we need to be able to collectively address our way of being and of interacting with the one another and our shared environment. Focusing on public policies alone without incorporating their psychosocial dimensions will continue to fall short of what is required to manage our future.

This is where Socio-Analytic Dialogue comes in.

Worldwide reactions to and country comparisons of societies' ability to address Covid-19 have brought to the forefront the importance of paying close attention to the underlying psychosocial issues from a systems dynamics perspective. As argued earlier working from a systems dynamics perspective at the country level is, in fact, what makes Socio-Analytic Dialogue distinct in both its mode of thinking and type of intervention from psychoanalysis; a field, notwithstanding our focus on large groups rather than the analytic dyad, from which several of its ideas are generated. Public policy making and country dialogue have traditionally ignored largely unconscious country-level social defenses. Nevertheless, Socio-Analytic Dialogue remains accessible to the world of public policy because the ways in which interventions are designed and implemented borrow from country dialogue approaches that are already widely used in promoting internalization of public policies.

While many may feel they understand the challenges the world is facing, this is unlikely to be fully the case. Not explicitly taking into account society-level unconscious defense mechanisms underpinning mental representations and resistance is likely to limit that understanding. This is what the unconscious, hence purposely hidden, implies.

In a nutshell, a country must first understand how it functions as a social system. This means to understand the nature and psychosocial purpose of the social defenses mobilized in response to anxieties. A country also needs to assess the quality and nature of "Object Relations" at the level of the entire society, meaning how various groups unconsciously relate to one another, to the State, and to their institutions. Disagreements about public policies are often the consequence of deeper psychosocial issues, which in turn are displaced into the public policy sphere. This kind of displacement (policies being easier to apprehend than largely unconscious psychosocial phenomena) often occurs because disagreements on policies allow for the underlying psychosocial dynamics to be verbalized.

The specificity of Socio-Analytic Dialogue is threefold:

1. It takes into account unconscious societal dynamics; these are the most resilient and difficult to understand;
2. It provides a rigorous approach to identify the social defenses (collective defense mechanisms mobilized by the society in response to anxieties); and
3. It prioritizes empathy-based dialogue and, as such, increases the propensity of subgroups in a society to positively identify with one another.

The most relevant contributions of Socio-Analytic Dialogue are twofold:

1. The idea that policies themselves can be used as social defenses; and
2. The importance of perverse societal dynamics in shaping policies and social outcomes.

The idea that policies themselves can be used as social defenses is totally absent in public policy. It goes a long way towards explaining confrontational psychosocial dynamics and resistance to change worldwide. It is also central to understanding the mechanisms underpinning the societal unconscious at work as well as its significant capacity to influence outcomes.

The role that perverse societal dynamics can play in shaping policies and social outcomes is rarely understood, if not completely ignored. Yet it is one of the most serious risks that we are confronted with today.

The Appendix to this book provides some of the theoretical background.

We now focus on two issues that are central to Socio-Analytic Dialogue's capacity to have an impact: reparative leadership and psychosocial transmission mechanisms.

Just to avoid any misunderstandings, psychosocial and systems dynamics approach is a complementary, albeit fundamental, intervention in support of more traditional and core ones such as public policy formulation, country dialogue, and civil society participation, including activism and political campaigns. To all of these, it brings a deeper, and until now essentially completely ignored, assessment of the psychosocial environment. This, in turn, is expected to decrease the severity of psychosocial roadblocks and facilitate reaching a common understanding. As repeatedly emphasized, it also creates meaning.

REPARATIVE LEADERSHIP

As clearly in evidence through the review of several country-level experiences, reparative leadership greatly facilitated the management of the Covid-19 pandemic. Although a psychoanalytic based approach to reparative leadership considers that it requires benevolent leadership, it may nevertheless be argued that under circumstances facilitating buy-in and identification, the Chinese authorities were also able to deliver results along the lines advocated here. This was facilitated by the fact that government actions that would have been seen as too coercive elsewhere were more palatable to the Chinese once a health emergency was declared. However, the Chinese leadership was unwilling to listen to warnings that were given early into the pandemic by Wuhan-based physicians. A more benevolent, humble and genuinely reparative leadership would not have experienced those warnings as attacks and, as a consequence, would likely have been more receptive.

The Covid-19 pandemic has, therefore, highlighted that reparative leadership is urgently needed. It is likely to decrease the propensity of regressed social defenses (e.g., scapegoating, splitting) to be mobilized since genuine reparative leadership, as seen in New Zealand, is capable of fostering empathic capability within a society.

Empathic capability is best achieved through Socio-Analytic Dialogue interventions capable of generating positive identifications between groups in a society. This brings feelings of shared meaning, no matter the extent to which a society might be split. It can, as such, become a prelude to dialogue in situations where it is thought to be elusive, including when groups demonize one another. Furthermore, empathic capability is more likely whenever groups are made aware of the existence and extent of unconscious collusions within a society. As seen earlier, there is little room for blame in a social system in which outcomes, once they have been experienced as shared responsibilities, become collectively owned. Empathic capability is a prerequisite to a nation's preparedness to work through some of its most salient psychosocial issues, particularly those concerning mourning. On many occasions, the strong wish to turn the page, seemingly as if nothing had ever happened, bodes poorly.

Working on empathic availability is not necessarily new. As part of the peace process implemented under the administration of President Santos in Colombia, encounters between ex-FARC guerilla members and victims or ex-paramilitaries regularly took place and had a positive impact on the society at large. The goal was to bridge seemingly irreconcilable divides by humanizing all sides as much as possible. This was meant to decrease the propensity for violence and cycle of revenge by allowing Colombian society to come to terms with issues such as biased mental representations, need for enemies, and demonization. Unfortunately, these initiatives were no longer promoted under President Duque, although some nevertheless continued at the community level. For example, demobilized FARC members are continuing to work with communities and even local police authorities to help in the fight against the pandemic. It is particularly noteworthy that this is taking place in spite of the significant erosion in basic trust due to the wave of killings of social leaders.[2]

The Covid-19 pandemic, and the type of systemic risks that it has forcefully brought to humanity's collective conscience should be a wake-up call. It should induce many societies to reflect on the need to function as appropriate containers. Understanding the world from a systems and psychosocial dynamics perspective might very well be the only way left to avoid increasingly predictable patterns of violence.

Reparative leadership capable of bridging seemingly irreconcilable divides by humanizing groups splitting from one another as much as possible has the power to decrease the propensity for violence. Such a leadership should be understood as intent on and capable of decreasing both the propensity of perverse societal dynamics to flourish and the propensity of regressed social defenses to be mobilized. It requires the promotion of a reflective society in the sense of it having the ability to understand—more precisely internalize-how it functions as a social system as defenses against anxieties. Reflective citizens, therefore, become aware of the nature and purpose of the social defenses mobilized by different groups as well as of the ways in which culture impacts shared thinking and assumptions (i.e., the societal unconscious). Understanding and approaching psychosocial dynamics from a judgment free position allow citizens to make sense of their psychosocial environment. This, in turn, creates new meaning, contributes to a society's aliveness and, as such, acts as a societal container.

Psychosocial dynamics, even if regressed, are the essence of a social system. A reparative leader in his/her role of communicating to the society the existing psychosocial dynamics can be thought of as an orchestra conductor allowing an audience to discover and appreciate music; the psychosocial dynamics in all their richness and complexity thought of as the music of the social system.

Furthermore, a society's reflectiveness can be significantly enhanced if special attention is given to existing unconscious collusions. Regardless of outcomes, they are almost certain to be present; groups often acting unconsciously on behalf of other groups. As also seen earlier, acknowledging unconscious collusions encourages a society to experience outcomes as a shared societal responsibility. In other words, the notion of blame and/or of guilt are absent whenever psychosocial dynamics are understood as being driven by the social system as a whole.

Understanding the psychic reality of each society's subgroups is key to enabling a society to develop empathic capability. This understanding of the other groups' psychic reality, where each group is given the possibility to experience it as if it were its own, is key to the promotion of positive identification between various groups at the level of an entire society. Positive identifications between society's groups are what set the stage for tolerance, compassion for others and empathic capability and availability at the level of the entire society. In such a social system, splitting is likely to decrease as mental boundaries between various subgroups start disappearing. This creates further meaning as a new and deeper sense of belonging is created.

What is described in the paragraph above is, incidentally, exactly what was beginning to develop in Colombia during the early implementation of the peace process. Sadly, this could not be sustained. The total disappearance of reparative leadership under the administration of President Duque in Colombia has almost surely translated into a worse management of the pandemic than would have been the case otherwise. While Colombia, as many countries without an adequate safety net, found itself in the unenviable situation of being in a position in which it could neither afford to maintain nor to end its lockdown, government's actions to restart the economy led to a massive reactivation of the virus' spread during the Spring and Summer of 2021. Furthermore, showing their contempt for the needs of their poorer constituents, several mayors were arrested on charges of corruption with coronavirus emergency funds.[3] And to make things worse, policy measures implemented in response to the Covid-19 pandemic were used as a pretext to weaken or withdraw protection for human rights defenders and social leaders.[4]

We now turn to psychosocial transmission mechanisms.

PSYCHOSOCIAL TRANSMISSION MECHANISMS

Thinking psychoanalytically about countries raises the important theoretical issue of psychosocial transmission mechanisms; in other words, how can a country begin the process of internalizing the ways in which it functions as a social system and, as a consequence, decrease the mobilization of regressed defenses throughout its society. This is a tall order but psychosocial transformations do occur. In general, those transformations have not, however, been the result of rigorous psychosocial evaluations and interventions and have had a greater propensity to be reversed.

Furthermore, we are undoubtedly witnessing a rapid increase in the mobilization of regressed social defenses worldwide. This, in turn, can only be mitigated by the systemic adoption of psychosocial and systems dynamics approach to public policy and country dialogue. This is especially important as we confront the post-pandemic world. It is important to act fast because societies' capacities to work through their own psychosocial dynamics were weakened during the pandemic.

Although Socio-Analytic Dialogue has never argued for applying psychoanalysis as it exists to a society since the societal unconscious would be inaccessible to interpretations, it does suggest that some psychoanalytic processes are relevant to public policy and social dialogue. For example, psychoanalytic-informed open listening at the societal level can only increase our ability to understand various groups' affects, communicate with one another, and question existing projections and introjections.

However, in most cases, psychosocial interventions can only be undertaken with small groups. Therefore, a major theoretical issue when working psychosocially at the country level is that of psychosocial transmission mechanisms. In other words, whether or not an entire society can be impacted in a fashion similar to that involving a small group. That would be the target of an intervention. There is no straightforward response to this as each situation has its own specificity.

Some interventions could be undertaken through the scaling up of interventions at the level of small groups. This was, for example, the case with Volkan (2006)'s work with refugees in Abkhazia (former Soviet republic of Georgia). He was able to make interpretations to an individual who, in turn, acted as a conduit for the interpretation to become internalized by the larger group. Volkan's remarkable fieldwork was the first to showcase explicitly a transmission mechanism for psychoanalytic-informed interpretations at the level of an entire group.

We now focus on interventions working directly at the level of the social system as a whole. This is best suited for public policy and country dialogue work. Morocco might not necessarily come to mind as a nation with the potential of working psychosocially on public policies and dialogue. And yet, OCP (*Office Cherifien des Phosphates*) its state-owned phosphate company led by a visionary and reparative leader has consistently encouraged innovation on the social front. As a result, the enterprise and its OCP foundation are behind the creation of a major university, a think tank, and several youth programs that rank among the most innovative in the world. Furthermore, it launched a new business philosophy, *Le Mouvement*, with the goal of promoting disruptive innovations by breaking with traditional management structures. From a psychosocial perspective, the launching of *Le Mouvement* is quite close in spirit to the free flowing and seemingly directionless processes that characterize psychoanalytic inquiry at the group level. Since its launch, a new mindset has clearly emerged and profoundly changed the way of thinking in the various communities impacted by the enterprise.

It is in this context that the OCP Foundation arranged for Socio-Analytic Dialogue to lead a process, through multiple meetings with youth groups affiliated with programs managed by either the foundation itself or by Mohammed VI Polytechnic University, aimed at "listening" to Moroccan youth. The process went very well and provided rich data on youth's aspirations, mental representations, and inner experiences of Moroccan society. While a large segment is undoubtedly desperately disenfranchised and angry, the majority of the groups Socio-Analytic Dialogue worked with, many participants coming from poorer households, highlighted that a large segment of Moroccan youth nevertheless feels quite positive about the future. To them, it only seems capable of improving.

The vibrant, hopeful and dynamic environment experienced in Morocco contrasted greatly with the sense of doom that seems to be more prevalent in several Western nations. While Morocco's cultural heritage predisposes the country quite well for such an initiative, there were nevertheless topics, such as corruption and power that were more prone to self- censorship. Yet it seemed that the authorities (at least at the level that Socio-Analytic Dialogue was working with) understood that psychosocial discussions on affects, regardless of the topic, were apolitical and non conducive to increasing the propensity for dissent. However, many young people, despite their optimism, expressed in a variety of ways how keen they were to leave the country through emigration abroad. However, contrary to what outside observers might have surmised, this did not imply that they wished to rebel against the social system. This seems largely due to the presence of the King who is experienced as a positive object of identification. As such, he acts as a container, strengthens Moroccan identity and renders the society more cohesive. All of this appears to make the latter more resilient to psychosocial shocks, which probably explains the success and solidarity that the nation demonstrated in its handling of the Covid-19 pandemic. Socio-Analytic Dialogue's work with Moroccan youth stopped shortly before the pandemic began. However, deepening the work by, for example, including outside groups (e.g., unemployed youth in the outskirts of Rabat or of Casablanca) would likely have required a buy-in from the authorities at a very high level. As a general rule, ownership at the highest level, the more so in nations where civil society's role might not yet be as overarching as elsewhere, is fundamental to prevent resistance and possible setbacks. Psychosocial processes everywhere remain fraught with complexities. Yet, increased internalization on the part of both civil society and governments of their relevance should increase the propensity for such processes to be implemented.

NOTES

1. "How to help the poorest through the lockdowns," May 3, 2020, https://www.ft.com/content/e851e3a2-8bbd-11ea-9dcb-fe6871f4145a.

2. Unfortunately, the goodwill of the FARC has been contrasted by the ongoing killing campaign of social leaders and former FARC members in Colombia, which even the pandemic could not dampen. See, the following video prepared by Rodeemos el Dialogo in Colombia. https://www.youtube.com/watch?v=S1xwJNlvh-U, May 20, 2020.

3. "Colombia arrests two mayors, seeks arrests of 8 more over corruption," *Colombia Reports*, May 22, 2020, https://colombiareports.com/colombia-arrests-two-mayors-seeks-arrest-of-8-more-over-coronavirus-corruption/.

4. "Colombia among world's worst performers in beating Covid-19," *Colombia Reports*, May 21,2020, https://colombiareports.com/colombia-among-worlds-worst-performers-in-beating-covid-19/.

Chapter 7

If Not Now, When? If Not You, Who?

Socio-Analytic Dialogue has already acquired vast experience working in settings as diverse as Latin America (Bolivia, Chile and Colombia, the latter during the peace process between the authorities and the *FARC*), the Maghreb (Tunisia after the onset of the Arab Spring and including with extremist youth and Morocco with Mohammed VI Polytechnic University), and Israel.

The analysis of the pandemic has clearly shown the importance of psychosocial dynamics in shaping outcomes. Understanding and taking into account psychosocial dynamics early would possibly have gone a long way towards preventing the abrupt changes in psychosocial environments that swept through Europe in November 2021 whereas violent protests erupted against the increasingly widespread required usage of health passes and the resulting exclusion of unvaccinated individuals. Ignoring psychosocial dynamics has led to splitting between groups, a social defense that is, in turn, skewing public health policy debates in favor of the adoption of rigid rules at the expense of adjusting policies based on public health criteria alone. As such, the situations in many European countries quickly reached breaking points whereas unacknowledged anxieties on all sides led to widespread rejections of containment measures and/or vaccines.[1]

The situation in the French Caribbean Island of Guadeloupe is particularly telling. In mid-November 2021, unusually violent protests erupted against the continued mandatory use of a health pass and the mandatory vaccination of health care workers; public policies implemented in the island mirroring by law those of continental France. Yet, the discontent expressed in the street quickly shifted to issues of economic fairness and exclusion, which shows how the rejection of the public health policies reflected—in displacement at first—a disavowal of the entire economic system of the island.

The psychosocial shock of the pandemic coupled with the increasingly undeniable realization of our collective inability to successfully tackle climate change make it imperative to incorporate psychosocial thinking into policy formulation and societal level dialogue. Humanity, possibly on the cusp of reaching a psychosocial point of no return, finds itself at a turning point. Psychosocial indicators of the latter include, for example, the rise in violence and even anti-Semitism in the German region of Saxony, where both Leipzig and Dresden are located. Saxony, which has the lowest rate of vaccination, is also the region where the Alternative for Germany, the rightist populist party, has its best results. Theories about vaccination making individuals sick or the virus not even existing became quite popular there. The graffiti and the signs carried at demonstrations in the region, some adorned with Nazi symbols and bearing anti-Semitic slogans such as "Covid is a Jewish lie" or referring to the Holocaust with "Impfen macht frei" (or Vaccination makes you free) are a testament to the downhill trajectory towards splitting and authoritarianism that the world risks embarking upon.[2]

We now continue by illustrating the psychosocial theoretical points referred to in the Appendix. The examples chosen for that purpose, one at the institutional level and one, Bolivia, at the country level, are what led to the Socio-Analytic Dialogue framework. Bolivia will always remain special to me as it turns out to have been the first time ever that a psychoanalytic study of a country and its policies was undertaken.

NARCISSISTIC DENIAL IN FOREIGN AID

The work, inspired by my own experience at the World Bank, was first presented at one of the International Study of the Psychoanalytic Study of Organizations (ISPSO) annual meetings and subsequently published in Boccara (2014). This work is of special importance to me as it is what led me, under the supervision of my first mentor in the field of psychosocial and systems dynamics, Laurence Gould, to begin my reflection into what later became Socio-Analytic Dialogue. While the topic was that of an organization, it also prepared me to embark on a journey thinking about country level psychosocial dynamics surrounding public policies since the World Bank, the organization that I wrote about, plays a significant role in public policies in a variety of aid-dependent countries.

In fact, years later the catastrophic management of the pandemic by many governments, in particular those from Western countries, often characterized by inconsistent and erratic policies turned out to share many similarities with the narcissistic denial fueled perverse psychosocial dynamics identified in the context of foreign aid. As such, it makes the latter particularly relevant to assessing and addressing the adverse developments observed during the pandemic.

Experiencing directly the psychosocial dynamics referred to above gave me the opportunity to experience first hand the pernicious and often unstoppable power of unconscious collusions. It had a profound impact on me, both from a personal and intellectual perspective. Looking back many years later, I can also say that it allowed me to understand what developing a profound empathic availability meant as, from my own perspective, I felt that there was essentially no blame to assign anywhere. In fact, what transpired was rarely the outcome of specific individuals enacting on behalf of the larger group's defensive needs a perverse attack on say a designated "bad" object. Instead, it was almost exclusively the outcome of complex and largely unconscious psychosocial dynamics. Incidentally, I had resigned a few years before to go work in financial markets and had recently been subsequently rehired. Unfortunately, the World Bank, as a social system, experienced resigning rather than applying for a leave of absence as a transgressive narcissistic attack. Retaliation, again in psychoanalytic terms, implied that I became "in the mind" one of the "contaminated" objects whose "assigned role," or psychosocial purpose they fulfilled, was to contain the anxieties that permeated the organization. These were the result of the World Bank, again as a social system, finding it increasingly difficult to maintain an idealized mental representation of itself.

As such, if one, in response, were to wish to indict "in the mind" the World Bank, it should only be about the institution as a social system (i.e., how it is impacted by mental representations, unconscious collusions, and social defenses) rather than anything else. Strangely enough, as exceedingly rare in those situations, I had the full support—and at the highest level—of the human resources department. Yet, this was nevertheless powerless to stop the psychosocial dynamics at play because the latter were deeply engrained and, as is always the case, fulfilled a defensive role for the struggling organization. Ultimately, my experience at the World Bank turned out to have a significant impact in allowing me to create what was to become Socio-Analytic Dialogue.

In a nutshell, the institutional romance, or shared mental representations, were an omnipotence fantasy of being chosen to save the rest of the world (i.e., foreign aid) and a grandiose fantasy associated with the prestige "in the mind" of the institution. As foreign aid's effectiveness became increasingly challenged, it became more difficult to maintain the romance and the institution mobilized social defenses in response to the anxieties created by both the omnipotence and the grandiose fantasies being challenged. See, Boccara (2014).

As also mentioned in the postscript on Afghanistan, this can occur in many institutions and for a variety of reasons. The defenses mobilized in return included splitting from the institution, denial, idealization as a way to shield oneself from a collective narcissistic injury, obsessiveness, and resistance to change. While these were largely unconscious, hence not fully known, their impact on the work quality and relationship with the clients could often be felt. The cost of ignoring these psychosocial dynamics (not that it was necessary deliberate) could therefore be high. This was the case in terms of client satisfaction (even if several of the countries are captive as they do not have alternative sources of financing) as well as staff morale; something that hurt productivity significantly due to a loss of meaning amongst Staff. These adverse psychosocial dynamics and their significant impact on the quality of the work could, however, have been significantly diminished had it been for a sustained and thorough internalization by Staff of the psychosocial dynamics defining the social system at the time.

The same applies to the baffling incompetence and sheer mediocrity with which several governments have managed the pandemic. It is likely that several of the organizational level defenses, including narcissistic denial, also played a role in explaining these outcomes.

UNDOING TRAUMAS IN BOLIVIA

As I was starting a series of psychosocial and systems dynamics informed discussions with policy makers, I was introduced by chance to Gonzalo Sanchez de Lozada, or "Goni," twice president of his native Bolivia; a transformative and historical figure for many, a polarizing individual and a symbol of the country's ills for others. The encounter led to in-depth exchanges between "Goni" and myself on the applicability of psychosocial ideas to societal transformation and leadership. Two years and several trips to Bolivia later, including work with high-level advisers to President Morales (mostly the key intellectual figures behind the *MAS*[3] movement), saw the publication of the first ever psychoanalytic-inspired analysis of a country and its public policies. See, Boccara (2013b). While the country remains split along political—and often ethnic—lines, this was less the case then than it has become now.

The analysis was able to explain how the shared mental representations of Bolivia, or "Bolivia in the Mind"; the guilt, shame, and wish to repair inherited from Potosi and the exploitation of silver; and the War of the Pacific with Chile, a chosen trauma,[4] led to the mobilization of social defenses that strongly impacted public policy choices and outcomes in Bolivia. The two most important social defenses included enactments to undo the trauma of Potosi (or, in displacement, the loss induced by the War with Chile), and a return to the pre-Colombian origins (as they are represented "in the mind"). Unsurprisingly, the latter is exactly what the election of President Morales represented to many.

As expected, the social defenses had a strong impact on the choices and implementation of public policies in Bolivia. One of the most important findings was the convergence of social defenses across groups seemingly diametrically opposed form one another historically, culturally, and economically. See, Boccara (2013b). In fact, the need to undo the original deed, the trauma of Potosi, was experienced particularly vividly in Bolivia. As a marker of identity, Potosi truly defines what is referred in Spanish to *Bolivianidad*, or the essence of Bolivian identity. Furthermore, it also seemed to be a much stronger marker of identity than the trauma of the Trans-Atlantic slave trade in Sub-Saharan Africa, including in West Africa, or than the Russian colonization of ex-Soviet Central Asian countries.

It is quite possible that implementing the kind of psychosocial work advocated in this book to Bolivia early on could have prevented the deepening splits that were sadly exacerbated towards the end of the Morales administration. In fact, this kind of work should have been implemented as early as with the administration of "Goni" Sanchez de Lozada who, in spite of actually empowering financially previously disadvantaged communities discriminated because of ethnic affiliation, nevertheless epitomized the extreme wealth of a few and the power of foreigners to steer the course of the country. His policies, regardless of how significantly they empowered indigenous communities (for the first time in Bolivian history), were hampered by mental representations of the leadership at the time. In fact, these policies paved the way for the election for the first ever president of indigenous descent. But Evo Morales tragically missed his *rendez vous* with history by moving away from deepening the reparative leadership that the country still needed. This deepened splitting and hate rather than allow Bolivia to mourn its past and move forward. See, Mesa Gisbert (2008).

For groups intensely split from one another in Bolivia, understanding the convergence of social defenses could possibly have gone a long way in allowing them to internalize the fact that their respective identities, that remain at the very origin of the splitting between them, were, in fact, much closer to one another than they routinely assumed. In creating shared meaning, Socio-Analytic Dialogue type interventions can increase the strength of the social compact.

CONCLUSIONS

While governments at the national level have yet to work systematically on public policy and country dialogue from a psychosocial and systems dynamics perspective, it can be done and is long overdue. Some preliminary work in the Kingdom of Morocco is another indicator of its feasibility and relevance.

In contrast, the developments in the United States, be it the management of the pandemic or the explosion of anger and frustration expressed by the Black Lives Matter (BLM) movement following the death of George Floyd, show the extent to which unacknowledged psychosocial issues can wreak havoc in a society. Floyd was an African American, who died at the hand of the Minneapolis police in May 2020. Naturally, it is not a coincidence that the movement exploded during the pandemic as anxieties were at an all-time high while failures in the system were becoming all too apparent This is probably a harbinger of things to come, there and elsewhere. It is not coincidental that commentators not associated with psychosocial and systems dynamics thinking are increasingly framing their arguments in terms that echo our thinking. See, Slaby (2020). This may signal an increased readiness worldwide to embrace those ideas. Yet applying them without the required rigor embedded in Socio-Analytic Dialogue would likely defeat the purpose as key defense mechanisms could easily be overlooked.

For example, little was said about unconscious collusions as well as what was projected on both the African American population and the security forces. The latter, just as any group in a society, can only introject what is projected onto them and sooner or later, the more so when anxieties are high, eventually act upon the "role" assigned to them. Rather than splitting and, as a consequence, seeing the police forces exclusively as a villain, it would likely have been more conducive to examine in-depth all the existing unconscious collusions so as to allow the nation as a whole to genuinely take collective ownership of institutionalized racism and its roots. While such an undertaking is far harder than simply looking at the splitting divide as that of BLM protesters and of the police, it is what is required. Such a divide certainly exists as African Americans have definitively bore almost the entire burden of police brutality and of racial injustice. While the psychosocial exercise is far more difficult since it prevents projecting blame outwards, it is the only way to move forward as a group. While the anger at the police forces might have been understandable, to be sustainable, profound reforms would likely require empathetic dialogue with all the key actors.

As argued earlier, working-through in the United States will likely not be easy. Yet the fact that social movements spearheaded by BLM were unusually widespread (not only cutting across racial groups but also, and far more revealing, even spreading to rural areas) suggests that disgust at the system might no longer be tolerated as it once was. Once this disgust becomes introjected as internalized shame, remaining silent becomes unbearable. Incidentally, it is when this introjection occurs (on a sufficient scale) that protest movements morph into major social movements. This is, for example, what genuinely triggered the Arab Spring in Tunisia. It is this kind of potentially significant changes in a psychosocial environment that highlights once more the relevance of psychosocial and systems dynamics thinking when confronted with events of the magnitude of the pandemic.

But this is nevertheless unlikely to be relevant to the United States; a society we had already characterized as incapable of promoting a genuine capacity for identification amongst its members. Thinking economically rather than psychosocially, neo-liberalism has transformed the society into a nation of entrepreneurs working exclusively for themselves. As such, there exists little capacity for relationships with others that are free of purpose. While freedom to act, albeit only as an entrepreneur, is seemingly unbounded (anyone in a country that enabled individuals such as Elon Musk or Jeff Bezos to strive can "technically" achieve anything), the neo-liberal society can nevertheless be coercive. See, Han (2017). Deeply internalized psychosocial mechanisms, that become self-imposed without much awareness have, until now, given neo-liberalism its endured stability. The sense of community, which is required for genuine transformation through collective actions to occur, has simply disappeared in most of the United States. Thus, it does not seem yet that the psychosocial shock brought about by the pandemic would be sufficient to alter the United States on that front.

However, besides rigorous psychosocial approaches, there can also be sporadic yet powerful actions that can have an impact. An impressive example of this is Ben McAdams, who as mayor of Salt Lake County went in disguise for three days as a homeless man (no one recognized him). He spent one night in the streets and one night in a shelter in order to experience first hand homelessness and understand why homeless individuals were so reluctant to stay in shelters. There is no way he could have accessed that information, no one would give it to him as a mayor. He witnessed the abuse perpetrated by shelters' staff. The mayor even had no intentions to disclose what he had done so that it would not be seen as a publicity stunt. This kind of commitment is impressive as it has the ability to change a situation that otherwise would be swept under the rug (homeless individuals are rarely a constituency of interest). It cannot however identify the psychosocial root causes of how homeless individuals are experienced, hence treated, by the general population. These are complex dynamics since homeless individuals, as outcast, will almost always be a repository of society's aggression and contempt.

More generally, while becoming increasingly diverse, most societies are nevertheless becoming more divided. These divisions decrease societal empathic capability since there is never a need to mobilize empathy for the "not us" with whom we never interact, except for asymmetric transactions (e.g., "interacting" with a store clerk or a cleaning staff). This takes us back to the importance of developing within societies the capacity for identification as a way to strengthen basic trust as well as the social compact.

In spite of the hugely traumatic experience of the pandemic, there is still hope in our collective ability to create a better future. The wide dissemination of the ideas in this book could be a catalyst toward the adoption of psychosocial and systems dynamics approaches to public policy and societal dialogue. This is a prerequisite to successfully addressing issues that may otherwise threaten humanity's future. Achieving a "good enough" degree of consensus may not be nearly as elusive as anticipated. Working along, rather than against, existing societal splits by recognizing them and even temporarily allowing them to be expressed, creates meaning in enabling all voices to be heard while suspending all judgments. Deliberately turning a blind eye by purposely not endeavoring to hear what is left unsaid is instead likely to worsen psychosocial dynamics by deepening rather than weakening splitting.

Governments and their civil society partners are, therefore, encouraged to begin systematically approaching policies and dialogue from a psychosocial and systems dynamics perspective. Socio-Analytic Dialogue interventions should be able to foster potentially far-reaching psychosocial transformations, including empathic capability at the country level; awareness and understanding of social defenses; and of country readiness to work through. This creates meaning.

Perverse societal dynamics must also be recognized. They can potentially prevent (or derail) governments adopting the type of approach recommended in this book. A crucial question is therefore whether these dynamics can also be addressed. While difficult at the individual level, it is not necessarily the case at the country level. In achieving meaning by emphasizing, and enabling internalization of greater public goods that transcend each individual, instrumentalism and transactional relations can be transformed into empathic capability. Last, psychosocial interventions at the country level often do not require the in-depth and lengthy processes that are the norms for psychoanalytic work at the individual level. Furthermore, in appealing to collective narcissism (e.g., national pride), changes in shared idealized mental representations, which define what a society strives for, can evolve in a robust fashion. See, Boccara (2014).

And, we conclude the book the way it began:

There comes a time when ideas potentially capable of profoundly changing the world must be brought to the centers of decision making. That time is now upon us.

NOTES

1. "Huge protests across Europe," November 22, 2021, https://www.bbc.com/news/world-europe-59363256 and "Violent clashes break out across Europe," November

22, 2021, https://www.rfi.fr/en/europe/20211122-violent-clashes-break-out-across-europe-as-demonstrators-protest-covid-restrictions.

2. "Anti-vaxxers and anti-Semites: welcome to Germany's COVID infection capital," November 23, 2021, https://www.haaretz.com/world-news/.premium.HIGHLIGHT.MAGAZINE-50-of-anti-vaxxers-voted-afd-a-visit-to-germany-s-infection-capital-1.10405789, and Reisler (2021).

3. *MAS* stands for the Movimiento al Socialismo, which is a left wing populist and indigenous political party founded in 1998 by Evo Morales, the former President of Bolivia.

4. See, Volkan (2004). A chosen trauma is defined as the collective mental representations of an event that has caused a large group to face losses, feel victimized, and share a humiliating injury. The mental representations of the trauma, or how the society chooses to remember it, become a marker of identity that link members of the society in a persistent sense of sameness throughout history.

Postscript

Socio-Analytic Dialogue and the Taliban

PREAMBLE

This book demonstrated how Covid-19 over the past two years was often approached with denial and the wish that it could be magically undone. This led to the costly management failures that we are seeing today. The text below, written shortly after the Taliban's entry into Kabul, has purposely not been updated to provide an example of a "here and now" psychosocial take on sensitive and rapidly evolving events as well as highlight the essence of what positive identification, a hallmark of Socio-Analytic Dialogue, is all about.

Socio-Analytic Dialogue focuses on entire societies at a deep level in order to take into account, as much as possible, societal unconscious aspects. From that perspective, the book argued that there was essentially no difference between Presidents Trump and Biden's approaches to the Covid-19 pandemic. The reason behind this is that the leadership will almost always act upon what is projected onto them by the social system. Therefore, while Americans are deeply split from one another, there was nevertheless convergence of affects and responses to Covid-19 at the psychosocial level. Observed behaviors are first and foremost a reflection of how a nation as a whole functions as a social system. As such, in the United States, Biden ended-up continuing Trump's inward-looking "America First" policy in spite of claiming otherwise with his "America is back" message that he was so keen to share with the Europeans. Incidentally, while this may appear to be counterintuitive at first, this should not necessarily come as a surprise. As indicated in chapter 6, previous work in Bolivia had already shown a psychosocial convergence between the leftist Morales administration and its predecessors from the right. See, Boccara (2013b).

On Afghanistan, the United States' failure, notably in planning its exit, likely also reflected the underlying social system. In fact, Biden and Trump's approaches on Afghanistan are not only similar but also turned out psychosocially to become an elusive search for a magical undoing. Thus, from a psychosocial perspective Biden's policies on both Covid-19 and Afghanistan were at the psychosocial level essentially identical. As such, I choose to include in the book a postscript on Afghanistan. The psychosocial convergence mentioned above shows the importance of thinking about policies from a psychosocial and systems dynamics perspective. This postscript uses the recent developments in Afghanistan to illustrate the importance and relevance of identification, even in cases, for example with the Taliban, where it might be the least expected. It is probably an understatement to say that Afghanistan is at a turning point since ending a 43 years conflict is now within reach. As is almost always the case, the psychosocial differences as to whether Afghanistan's new chapter will be a success or a failure are small. The path ahead will not be easy. Yet positive identification grounded on a profound psychosocial understanding of all the parties involved could go a long way towards Afghanistan embarking successfully on a new course.

To this we now turn.

POSITIVE IDENTIFICATION IN THE LAND OF THE LONE JEW

I had initially thought of "I too could have been a Taliban" as the title of this postscript. The idea was to convey in striking terms that genuine positive identification, aiming to experience for oneself in a completely unhindered way the psychosocial experience of the "Other," is not only fundamental but also particularly relevant at a time when it is likely to seem the most out of reach. This would be to take the ideas of Shapiro (2019) at heart, to ask, as a global citizen, "how is the other right?" Yet, I feared such a title could be misinterpreted and judged too provocative in the West following the harrowing images of crowds of Afghans at the airport in Kabul desperately seeking to flee the country. It is also unlikely that the United States, as a social system, would have the capacity to tolerate such an identification at a time when the resounding failure of its strategy became so apparent to the entire world. Furthermore, with its extraordinarily rich heritage and culture, mental representations of Afghanistan should not be solely limited to the Taliban.

As such, I chose to focus instead on a unique fact about the country. At the time of this writing, it only had one Jewish inhabitant, Zabulon Simintov who, in spite of having been given the option to be evacuated, chose to remain in what had just become the Islamic Emirate of Afghanistan. And the startling story does not end here. While the Taliban had imprisoned Zabulon Simintov before, the group indicated that he had nothing to fear; something that was likely to hold this time around. Furthermore, upon his refusal to leave, allegedly to avoid being prosecuted in Israel, as he would not grant his wife a divorce under Jewish law, the team that was sent to rescue him managed to airlift some of the players of the Afghan national women soccer team. After completion of this postscript, it was revealed that the lone Jew left Afghanistan on September 7, 2021. While he did not fear the Taliban, he reluctantly went into exile out of fear of the Islamic State Khorasan capturing and killing him. I nevertheless maintained the title of this postscript since Afghanistan was the land of the lone Jew for more than sixteen years from 2005 until Zabulon's departure.

As I had just finished writing a first draft of the book on the psychosocial aspects of the Covid-19 pandemic, the world was confronted with what are likely to become defining images of the Western intervention in Afghanistan, in particular the footage of Afghans running alongside a US Air Force plane taking off from Kabul with at least two individuals who were clinging to the plane falling to their death after it taking off. These horrific scenes of desperation will be etched in our collective memory for a long time to come.

The United States' hasty withdrawal symbolizes perfectly the utter failure of its strategy in Afghanistan since it began supporting the Mujahedeen against the communist government and then the Soviet Union in 1979. The naïve splitting between good and evil that more often than not permeates Americas' childish mental representations of the world is so striking that those that would ultimately give birth to the Jihadist movements of tomorrow could only be seen as freedom fighters in response to their opposition to then Reagan's Evil Empire (i.e., the USSR). And yet, it was the communist regime in Afghanistan that was in the process of liberating and empowering Afghan women, a far cry from what were then the already known views of the Mujahedeen. Yesterday's "good objects," the Taliban were even seen as a major ally in the War on Drugs, quickly morphed into "bad objects" par excellence after September 11, 2001, in light of the fact that Al-Qaeda's leadership was based in Afghanistan under the protection of the Taliban.

Driven by the psychosocial imperative of repairing its significantly damaged societal narcissism, the United States, traumatized by the September 11, 2001 attacks on its home soil, found itself ill-prepared to confront the complex psychosocial dynamics that awaited it in the war-torn nation of Afghanistan. The United States intensely split mental representations embedded in "*Every nation in every region now has a decision to make: Either you are with us or you are with the terrorists*,"[1] augured poorly for the decisions that followed as part of the so-called War on Terror. The latter is a misnomer that speaks volume to the grandiose fantasies that must have permeated the United States as a social system, hence a large share of its decision makers, at the time. It is important to note that while the Bush administration drove the decisions, it also acted in response to what was projected onto it. While social systems can be influenced by politics, the largely unconscious psychosocial mechanisms that drive collective behaviors are often deeply embedded and, as such, much less driven by politics than by mental representations, anxieties, and social defenses.

The United States, in response to its psychosocial needs of portraying and experiencing its intervention in Afghanistan in a narcissistically gratifying manner, was prone to either misunderstand the subtleties of the psychosocial dynamics on the ground or deliberately misrepresent them to the public. For example, the web of relationships that exist between Afghan forces on opposite sides of one another remained opaque to them. Yet, kinship and tribal connections in Afghanistan allowed tribal elders to create safe spaces where opposing factions could meet and reach settlements in a bid to avoid violence. It also explains the Taliban's unhindered advance and the speedy fall of Kabul. These arrangements act as an insurance policy since a family will often have sons belonging to groups fighting with one another. Incidentally, these arrangements are also sanctioned in Islam, as seen for example with the following surah from the Quran, "*We have not created the heavens and the earth and everything in between except for a purpose. And the Hour is certain to come, so forgive graciously.*"[2] The refusal, out of hubris, to recognize mistakes that were repeatedly made in the past augurs poorly for the future. This is, however, the stance adopted by the Biden administration and NATO. Both chose to explain the stunning debacle by focusing solely on the fact that the former Afghan administration and army chose not resist the Taliban.

In any case, Western nations did not have the welfare of the Afghans in mind. Development is almost never a byproduct of war. The reliance on warlords that could be more brutal than the Taliban and the resulting abuses in human rights (including by US Special Forces) sealed the fate of Afghanistan early on. Revenge often occurs in civil wars whenever the distribution of power is altered, the more so if there is foreign interference. It was also likely that mental representations of a nation impoverished and traumatized by years of war in a region that is also a major player in the international drug trade played a role. Many outside actors probably internalized, a reflection of their own biased mental representations, that the suffering that history had inflicted on the fiercely proud and independent people of Afghanistan was the only fate that they could achieve on their own. The more this was the case, the more the interactions between Afghans and non-Afghans, also a reflection of widespread negative biases against Muslim societies, would become dominated by condescending arrogance on the part of the latter.

This is not to say that opportunities were not created during the last twenty years, far from it. Education was widely expanded, including to girls to whom it had been completely denied. Jobs that women could also hold were created and civil society was able to have a voice. But overall, security deteriorated and the drug trade exploded. This, de facto, transformed the country into a narco state; something that could have been anticipated given what was already known before the war. See, Ludwig (2021). The huge sums of money made available to government officials, contractors, Warlords, and NGO's led to corruption on a grand scale. In the words of David Davis, former British Secretary of State for Exiting the European Union and Member of Parliament since 1997, "*The harsh truth is that we had no strategy . . . government officials and their families became remarkably rich quickly . . . The UK, USA, and their allies have installed and supported a corrupt state.*"[3]

As stated in the executive summary of the 11th SIGAR (Special Inspector General for Afghanistan Reconstruction) report, "*Lessons from twenty years of Afghanistan reconstruction*"[4] published a few days before the Fall of Kabul, "*U.S. government has now spent 20 years and $145 billion trying to rebuild Afghanistan, its security forces, civilian government institutions, economy, and civil society. The Department of Defense (DOD) has also spent $837 billion on the war . . . While there have been several areas of improvement—most notably in the areas of health care, maternal health, and education—progress has been elusive and the prospects for sustaining this progress are dubious*." Incidentally, Brown University's Cost of War project estimates the DOD figure to be even higher, at 2.26 trillion when including veterans' disability and medical costs, interest on borrowing, and other factors. But the war in Afghanistan was far from a failure from the perspective of the major defense contractors in the United States, whose boards of directors include retired top-level military officers. Thus, while the total return on the S&P 500 over the last twenty years was 517 percent, it was 1,236 percent for Lockheed Martin and 1,196 percent for Northrop Grumman.

The stories above truly show the extent to which America and its allies' involvement in Afghanistan was a catastrophic failure of strategy. And yet, it should not come a surprise. The kind of developments briefly mentioned were well known and well understood by most of the parties involved. While there were vested interests that can explain the situation (war is profitable), this cannot be and is not the whole story. The costs of failure far outweighed the benefits to the few. Furthermore, the United States had no incentive incurring the consequences that such an outcome would have on its prestige and influence worldwide. Thus, something else must also have been at play.

Once again, the answers can be found in psychosocial and systems dynamics. At the organization level (e.g., DOD, the Department of State and the myriads of contractors and development practitioners that went to work "in the field"), the issues are, in general, well understood. Understanding the specific mechanisms through which psychosocial dynamics in situations like these impact policy outcomes often takes us to perverse organizational dynamics. The latter are key to understanding corrupt and abusive behaviors that were often the hallmark of the interactions, military or not, between the Western nations and Afghanistan. See, Long (2008) and Boccara (2014). Some of the most important psychosocial aspects related to perversion in organizations are narcissism, denial in order to maintain an idealization based on fantasized mental representations, and the need for accomplices in order to turn a blind eye to what is happening. The latter is called collusive denial. It is almost certain that it was the most important psychosocial mechanism that led to the US failure. As argued in Boccara (2014), development assistance, with its shared fantasies as repair acts, of "saving the rest of the world" is particularly prone to the kind of psychosocial dynamics mentioned above. The same would likely apply to foreign armed forces in Afghanistan whose mission was coached in grandiose terms with: 1) destroying evil for the good of humanity as part of the War on Terror; and 2) lifting the country out of poverty as part of Afghanistan's reconstruction. Collusive denial is likely to have been the single most important psychosocial mechanism at play within the armed forces, the contractors, and even Non-Governmental Organizations (NGO's). This, in turn, likely led to all sorts of abuses; not solely of human rights (those almost always occur, the more so in asymmetrical conflicts) but also in profiteering from aid (excessively large sums of money were available in comparison to the country's level of income). But, perverse behaviors are, because of their uncomfortable truths, almost always denied. As a consequence, shirking of responsibilities and abusive practices often became the norm. In such a psychosocial environment, individuals such as contractors[5] or development assistance personnel would likely have colluded in focusing on the material benefits (and for some, prestige) while disregarding the main purpose of them being there. In other words, their primary task would have corroded if not completely lost.

The above, based on my experience working with organizations, is not meant whatsoever to be a psychosocial analysis of the various types of organizations that were involved in Afghanistan under the auspice of the US government. While the assumptions may very well hold, the sole intent here is to illustrate psychosocial and systems dynamics thinking and its relevance. In the case of the United States' involvement in Afghanistan and the War on Terror, a psychosocial analysis of what September 11 meant; a psychosocial understanding of the mental representations in the United States of

Afghanistan and of the Taliban; a psychosocial understanding of how the United States perceived itself and its role in the world (actual and wished for); and, last, detailed psychosocial and systems dynamics analysis of the various organizations that were involved would all together have gone a long way towards improving outcomes. The extent of the likely significant negative mental representations of Afghans and of the various actors involved in Afghanistan probably complicated the tasks significantly. After all, the installation of both a new government and the beginning of development assistance were concomitant with the creation and transfer of prisoners, the so-called "worst of the worst," to Guantanamo. While these two aspects of the United States' involvement with Afghanistan might have been intended to be entirely distinct in both implementation and staff involved, they were nevertheless "in the mind" associated with one another at the level of the entire social system. As such, our premise is that the task the United States, as a social system, imposed upon itself, was essentially impossible to perform without the support of psychosocial and systems dynamics analysis. Once again, we were faced with an elusive wished-for magical undoing, which is what the War on Terror, in response to the trauma of September 11, 2001, was supposed to accomplish.

Therefore, the pairing of Afghanistan with War on Terror is almost impossible not to be psychosocially extraordinarily symbolic. And this holds for both sides of the divide, Taliban and coalition countries, as well as for the majority of Afghans. Grandiose fantasies (we won), unbearable shame (we lost), relief that it is over, and extreme fears for the future are all bound to coexist. These seemingly irreconcilable psychosocial dynamics all have their source in the swift return of the Taliban to power in August 2021. To the Taliban, we, therefore, now turn.

Regardless of the many reassuring comments the Taliban have repeatedly made since entering Kabul, it remains, at this stage, very difficult not to associate the Taliban with the reign of terror that they had imposed earlier. Women, in particular, were stoned to death, whipped in public, coerced into forced marriage, banned from working or attending school, and not allowed to venture outside unless accompanied by a male relative and forced to wear a burka.

While it is still too early to know what to expect, it could very well be that the Taliban will relax its grip on women out of necessity. They now have to manage an economy that is close to free fall and doing so successfully requires human capital. The latter is in extremely short supply, the more so following the large number of mostly well-educated Afghans that managed to be exfiltrated from the country by the allied nations that fought the Taliban. In fact, in rural areas controlled by the Taliban over several years, women doctors and nurses were allowed to continue, and provide access to health care to women that would not come to a clinic otherwise. Yet many women appear to be genuinely afraid of what the future holds for them in an Afghanistan governed by the Taliban. The urban and most educated women feel that the worse is yet to come; their life as they have known it until now having basically ended.[6] For example, although a decision she wished she could have avoided, Zarifa Ghafari, who is only 27 years old but became in 2018 the first woman mayor in Maidan Shahr, a remote corner of Afghanistan's Paktia province, ended-up fleeing the country as she feared being killed by the Taliban. The same despair can also be found amongst young men as witnessed, for example, by Zaki Anwari's fate, the teenager who played for the national youth football team and who fell to his death from the US Air force plane that took off from Kabul on August 16, 2021. After all, as underlined by Wassim Nasr, "*the new head of their* [the Taliban] *political office, Mullah Abdul Ghani Baradar, spent eight years in prison in Pakistan. He was a close friend of the former Taliban leader Mullah Omar. The group's new No. 2, Sirajuddin Haqqani, belongs to the militant Haqqani network, which has close ties to al-Qaida. And the recently appointed governor of Khost, Mohammad Nabi Omari, spent 12 years in Guantanamo and was only released thanks to a trade that was made for a U.S. hostage.*"[7] Therefore, the actors, and almost certainly their ideology, remain unchanged. While this, in itself, does not imply that they have not changed, it seems unlikely. Yet, nothing whatsoever should preclude engaging with them psychosocially and to jointly explore differences.

While Abdul Balkhi, from the Taliban cultural commission, indicated in the first official interview from the Taliban since they entered Kabul that their approach would be "*enforcing law on others but enforcing it on ourselves and then giving it as an example for society to follow suit*," this may not be enough. In the same interview, he also indicated—as had been emphasized on several occasions—that the Taliban would not compromise on the application of Sharia Law, which is the law of the land. While it appears to be the case that the Taliban will indeed enforce laws on themselves first, their application of Sharia Law, even if "fair," would nevertheless likely reinforce feelings amongst some Afghans, particularly women, that the society prevents them to live a fulfilling life. While such feelings are mostly driven by societal norms, laws and their interpretations can and often have a huge impact. Working through collectively the extreme suffering that was inflicted on the people of Afghanistan by years of conflict, making significant progress on alleviating extreme poverty could be hampered by the Taliban's views on women's role in a society. Whether or not those views are required in Islam is, of course, an extremely delicate point, particularly to the Taliban. Such views would need to be thought through and addressed with all the subtleties and mutual respect that this requires.

In the meantime, it is important to acknowledge and remain aware that the allied countries never invaded Afghanistan for the sake of protecting women's rights. As stated earlier, the Communist party supported women's rights and emancipation while the United States championed the Mujahedeen in light of the imperatives of the Cold War. Since, the first and foremost rationale for the war in Afghanistan was the War on Terror, even if varied economic development and human rights objectives were nevertheless used to justify and even romanticize the allied interventions, few genuinely cared for women's rights in Afghanistan.[8]

Regardless of what is assumed to be the Taliban's stance on individual freedom and human rights, one should not unequivocally close all doors and justify it along the same lines that alternative justifications (other than terrorism) were given for continuing intervening in Afghanistan. The use of the word regardless at the beginning of the previous sentence is again meant to convey the complete neutrality with which identification takes place. In what is a position of humbleness, one's own views do not and should not matter. They are not of interest as what is at stake are the people of Afghanistan and ways in which their welfare may be impacted. Self-imposed and genuine narcissistic withdrawal matters. Thus, one should always strive to unconditionally prioritize working psychosocially so as to genuinely understand—in a complete judgment free approach—the underlying psychosocial dynamics at play and aim to explore ways in which, thanks to mutual respect, progress can be made. While there is no guarantee that meaningful progress can be achieved, empathic identification can go a long way in creating a safe space to discuss sensitive issues, notably those pertaining to identity.

For example, Iyad el Baghdadi, a West Bank Palestinian activist and writer living in the Gulf states and then exiled at the onset of the Arab Spring to Norway, tweeted, "*I can tell you with the wisdom of hindsight that a lot of it is really about identity and very little of it is about spirituality. We feel humiliated by the West, and alienated from our own pre-colonial identities*." While his experience may have little, if anything, to do with that of the Taliban, his words nevertheless echo my experience and that of a Tunisian psychoanalyst working with radicalized Tunisian youth. As Ben Smaïl and Boccara (2015) indicate in their psychosocial analysis of the Islamic State, "*joining Daesh is a defense against the severe narcissistic injury inflicted on a disenchanted and humiliated youth . . . Daesh seems capable to transcend cultures, perhaps even religions . . . jihadist videos . . . less prone to mention God but often have perverse societal dynamics . . . figure prominently in their message*." It is not implied in any way whatsoever that these same affects also exist with the Taliban. The above is only meant as an example to illustrate the explanatory power of otherwise almost always ignored psychosocial dynamics. The Taliban's experience with a brutal and lengthy conflict in their impoverished homeland for over forty years is not something Islamic State recruits, particularly those from outside Iraq, had experienced in a similar fashion.

In what follows, we argue that at the psychosocial level, engagement with the Taliban is the preferred option and, at the very least, one very much worth attempting. While it is understandable that the opposite stance, including economic sanctions, be considered by some, history suggests, as was the case with I.R. Iran, that this is often counterproductive. While moral imperatives may be raised, they are often applied selectively. Afghanistan is unfortunately poised to be one of those countries whose history makes it hostage to a credibility gap; something that should be unfathomable as the country is already likely on the brink of famine. What follows illustrates how psychosocial and systems dynamics would be applicable to a country like Afghanistan, particularly as the nation finds itself for the first time in more than four decades in charge of its own destiny.

Our starting point is, as always, genuine identification devoid of any specific purpose. In other words, we suggest endeavoring seeing, as in experiencing, the world from their perspective, and nothing else. This identification has to be ex-ante rather than ex-post. This implies that empathic identification is the starting position rather than something that would be the outcome of any interactions. As such, it becomes unconditional. It starts from a position of eagerness to know rather than to judge. This is absolutely fundamental. By being ex-ante, the identification implies absolutely nothing about supporting or not supporting the Taliban. Were it to be ex-post instead, hence based on interactions first, it would suggest that neutrality, neither supporting nor rejecting the Taliban, no longer holds.

With those caveats, we are now able to return to what was initially felt earlier to be too provocative:

"I too could have been a Taliban."

Having the audacity to accept and state this, crossing with just one sentence what to most is an irreconcilable divide, should be interpreted as a mark of profound respect. Once again, the "could have been" above is precisely meant to convey identification, which says nothing about adhesion. Although seemingly powerful, the statement above is also simply true just by virtue of its logic; anyone born in Afghanistan and experiencing what some of the Taliban fighters did could have made the same choices. But the opposite is also true. Identification, therefore, allows one, as well as those one identifies with, to explore a state of mind and its opposite. As such, identification is powerful as it not only signals a complete readiness to hear the story of the "Other" but also places one in a position to be heard by that "Other." This is the meaning of what is suggested: a collective journey, acting as a repair act, whereas all sides can begin exploring one another's mental representations—actual and wished for—and one another's anxieties. While some core values that are at the foundation of the Taliban project, may be set in stone, there are many issues, in fact most, that could be successfully explored jointly in the respectful and empathetic environment that identification enables.

While, as argued earlier, the extent to which the Taliban might have evolved remains unknown, there seems to be little doubt that their understanding of the world has changed. They are also probably aware of the challenges of managing a country with a population, especially in Kabul, that has been exposed to opportunities and ideas that were simply not accessible in 1996 when they first took power. While Internet access remains limited, many Afghans have access to messaging services. Sadly, recent developments, be it the United States freezing the country's foreign reserves deposits held at the Federal Reserve, the cancellation of balance of payments support by the International Monetary Fund and of development assistance by the World Bank suggest that the economy is almost certain to collapse quickly. As a consequence, millions of Afghans may soon face starvation due to the conflict, drought, and the Covid-19 pandemic. As such, the UN has called for urgent financial support to Afghanistan.

The Taliban's eagerness to succeed in the face of the daunting obstacles identified above suggests that there could be psychosocial entry points allowing for genuine and respectful dialogue. This does not imply—nor should it—that the Taliban will act the way the Western world would prefer. While they encouraged all public sector employees to go back to work, several female anchors were barred from their jobs on state TV. Furthermore, the general amnesty, as part of the national reconciliation proclaimed by the Taliban may have been accompanied by door-to-door searches outside Kabul to look for collaborators and, in some cases, kill them. There are also allegations of violence against those perceived to be or identified as homosexuals.

But Afghanistan is far from having the monopoly on human rights violation. Serious human rights violation and terrorism are on the rise and spreading in regions such as Western Africa coastal countries south of the Sahel or Mozambique that had, until recently, been immune from those threats. This has not precluded the rest of the world from engaging with those countries. Thus, until proven otherwise, it still seems that engagement, particularly at the psychosocial level, is the preferred route. In fact, this is what some Afghans that know all too well the risks and have the most to lose from the Taliban have been advocating. For example, Fazl Hadi Wazin, who ran for Vice President in 2020, urged the international community to put the Taliban to the test rather than outright rejecting them; a view that was also expressed by Germany's chancellor Angela Merkel. It is precisely because the Taliban are at a turning point in their history, winning the war being a lot easier than governing a country, that now is the time to cautiously engage with them; not only on policy issues but also at the psychosocial level. If anything, the tragedy at the time of this writing with the death of 13 US soldiers and, at least, 169 Afghan civilians on August 26, 2021, reinforces this point; the Taliban themselves having to confront terrorism. Thus, as strange as this may seem, it could be that the international community would be working with the Taliban to limit the spread of terrorism. Yet, while this might apply within Afghanistan, it is unlikely to hold outside the country's borders. The Taliban's victory against the United States, which is how many Islamist groups perceive it worldwide, provides a huge impetus to many of those groups to defy the West further.

As such, one could conceive, even if it may seem unrealistic for now, engaging the Taliban psychosocially to encourage them to demonstrate, as a gift to the world, ways in which social policies based on an understanding of the values embedded in Islam may have the potential to improve social compacts, connectedness, and genuine solidarity between individuals. This type of engagement is a mark of profound respect, in the sense of inviting them, rather than focusing on denouncing their "backwardness," to contribute to solutions to shared problems. This could possibly open some doors to an improved mutual understanding and also a softening of their positions as they are brought to recognize everyone's potential and humanity. And yet, it will also be necessary to give them the space they need to work through their own psychosocial issues. As Afghans, they too have suffered greatly and been traumatized. The Taliban can evolve, incidentally a viewpoint also shared by the Combating Terrorism Center of West Point,[9] and become a genuine opportunity for Afghanistan to successfully emerge from years of conflicts and manag its own destiny.

Orientalism and romanticization of the West as a savior of culturally underdeveloped nations has not only been rarely beneficial but also been used to justify devastating military operations. Afghanistan, with its hugely important geostrategic location, is no exception. As the US choosing to withdraw signals, the time has come to turn the page on the self-defeating romance of Western occupation for the benefits of the local population. Instead engaging all parties psychosocially without pre-conditions or specific objectives could go a long way towards a collective healing. Therefore, the time is now upon us to engage Afghanistan and the Taliban in ways that have until now been deliberately shunned. An earlier adoption of a psychosocial and systems dynamics approach to the West's interactions with Afghanistan would possibly have had the potential to change the course of history.

There undoubtedly are several important psychosocial issues that could—and likely should—be explored if the Taliban, the soon to be constituted government of Afghanistan, and civil society (were it to be possible to launch such an initiative) were at some point keen to reflect on Afghanistan and nation building from a psychosocial and systems dynamics perspective.

While it may be premature to start thinking along those lines, the issues of interest could only be defined with the different parties. The process itself would naturally be endogenous since whenever topics previously brought up in Socio-Analytic Dialogue working groups would be considered to be sufficiently worked through, other topics would likely surface and be included in the workshops. Likely topics could, for example, include for the Taliban working though feelings surrounding their recent success. The latter may not only include grandiosity since they are back in power and are seen by many outsiders as having vanquished the United States but also fear and apprehension as they now have to manage an unusually difficult social and economic situation. They also may have to let go and mourn some of their past identity if they wish, as they have repeatedly indicated, to adapt to Afghanistan's changed social landscape since they last were in power while keeping what to them are core principles. This is, of course, psychosocially fraught with complexities. It may also require distancing themselves from ideas that may be experienced for now as Western concepts but yet re-appropriating those for themselves in ways that are compatible with a strengthening rather than a weakening of their identity. Generosity and empathy in victory would go a long way towards healing the society. What holds for the Taliban also holds for other members of Afghan society since the 1996–2001 period during which the Taliban were in power was hugely traumatic for many. Feelings of shared identity being under attack in a world, which they have perceived as hostile for a very long time, will also need to be worked through. Furthermore, the entire nation is traumatized by years of conflict, including for some incarceration and torture. While the latter adds complexity, victims can also be extraordinarily empathetic in response to the suffering that they have been through and, if they have been able to, worked through. These are just a few thoughts to illustrate the kind of issues that are likely to be relevant.

As is the case with psychosocial and systems dynamics thinking, the approach would focus on small group psychosocial meetings with various members of the society to explore mental representations and the mobilization of collective defenses. The latter will play a defining role in determining whether the forthcoming Afghan government will be successful at allowing Afghanistan to manage the aftermath of the protracted conflicts it endured. Participation of some members of the Taliban senior leadership would be key to ensure that they do not fall prey to large group (i.e., at the country level) unconscious dynamics, including those at the level of its leadership and of its ranks and file units, that they cannot be fully aware of otherwise. Introspection following such momentous events can only benefit them and the society. Such working through is slow but critically important. As Long (2018) indicates, "Manic reparation, a simple wish to repair out of guilt alone does not hold. Long-term reparation requires a true recognition of otherness on all sides."

NOTES

1. President Bush's address to a joint session of Congress and the nation on September 20, 2001, https://www.washingtonpost.com/wp-srv/nation/specials/attacked/transcripts/bushaddress_092001.html.

2. Surah Al-Hijr, *Holy Quran* 15:85.

3. Interview given to *Conservative* Home, August 16, 2021, See, https://www.conservativehome.com/platform/2021/08/david-davis-afghanistan-and-america-2-the-harsh-truth-is-that-we-had-no-strategy-and-fell-back-on-supporting-a-corrupt-state.html.

4. Special Inspector General for Afghanistan Reconstruction report, August 2021, https://www.sigar.mil/pdf/lessonslearned/SIGAR-21-46-LL.pdf.

5. Many of the contractors were military mercenaries used to avoid applicable norms of international warfare.

6. "An Afghan Woman in Kabul: Now I have to Burn Everything I Have Achieved," *The Guardian*, August 15, 2021, https://www.theguardian.com/world/2021/aug/15/an-afghan-woman-in-kabul-now-i-have-to-burn-everything-i-achieved.

7. See, https://www.spiegel.de/international/world/terror-expert-on-afghanistan-the-real-threat-is-islamic-state-not-al-qaida-a-c2529e57-0e1c-4d57-8bc9-bbc69c0ad71d, August 27, 2021.

8. "Les Etats Unis n'ont pas Envahi l'Afghanistan pour Sauver les Femmes," *Solidaire*, August 17, 2021, https://www.solidaire.org/articles/malalai-joya-les-etats-unis-n-ont-pas-envahi-l-afghanistan-pour-sauver-les-femmes?fbclid=IwAR0LkFms9YV9COqVJkU6NxtZg-QMEGB2uyiOEDFoxeRj5vHlFNjqLVinFnU. Interview given by Malalai Joya, who is often thought as the most influential woman of Afghanistan. A well-known Afghan activist, she was a member of parliament who denounced vehemently the role of Warlords following US intervention.

9. "Have the Taliban Changed?," *Combating Terrorism Center Sentinel*, Volume 14, Issue 3, March 2021, https://ctc.usma.edu/have-the-taliban-changed/.

Appendix

Main Theoretical Notions Underpinning Socio-Analytic Dialogue

The appendix is based on what was first presented in the Socio-Analytic Dialogue blog, socioanalyticdialogue.org and published in Boccara (2013a) and in Boccara (2014).

Several concepts are useful to help representative groups to express their psychosocial experience of the society and allow for psychosocial conclusions to be drawn. However, similarly to what takes place in an analytic dyad, the work is unique each time (no standard approach) and is defined by the underlying issues as well as governments and civil society' areas of interest. In fact, it does not really matter where one starts, as sooner or later, anxieties and other psychosocial issues will likely be expressed. As always, it is important to pay attention to the psychosocial data that allows one to infer and, of course, validate what is not being said.

The goal is to understand how a nation functions as a social system, in other words, the nature and purpose of the social defenses mobilized against anxieties. Last, a fundamental aspect of the work, once psychosocial issues have been inferred and validated, is internalization; the latter a prerequisite to working-through.

What follows introduces some of the key concepts relevant to Socio-Analytic Dialogue.

SOCIO-ANALYTIC MAP OF THE COUNTRY

The notion of social systems as defense against anxieties or social defenses is probably the most important psychosocial concept of which policy makers should be made aware. The main idea is that the needs of members of a group to deal with anxieties lead to the development of a social system, which becomes an intrinsic part of the structure, culture, and mode of functioning of the group. The defenses operate mostly unconsciously, the social system the result of largely unconscious collusive interactions between members of the group. The concept can be extended to a society and its culture. Projective identification can induce a group, even a country, to take on the role that others, unconsciously, wish for it to adopt. Taken together, social defenses and projective identification are capable of explaining otherwise seemingly irrational societal dynamics surrounding public policies.

Understanding the psychosocial issues at play in a country requires identifying and understanding its inhabitants' emotional experiences pertaining to their environment, meaning:

1. The internal representations that inhabitants have of their country (how they view their country) and the kind of nation that they are aspiring to (their ideal); and
2. The inter-groups projections and introjections (how subgroups in the country view others and how they respond to how others view them) and their behavioral implications.

This constitutes the Socio-Analytic Map of the Country. The degree of stratification chosen is a function of the homogeneity of the society and of the psychosocial issues of interest. The idea of a map suggests that it might be possible—as a form of dialogue—to "travel" along the various projections and introjections, allowing members of a country to better understand the experience of the various "Others" that constitute their society.

From a psychosocial perspective, ways by which the various subgroups interact in society are the projections and introjections. Projection here is used in a general sense, meaning how one group sees another. This definition includes the more specific case, which is the rigorous psychoanalytic definition, of a projection as the outcome of a displacement of unwanted parts of the self/group into an object (e.g., another group). Selecting a broader and simpler definition, in order to use it at the country level, allows Socio-Analytic Dialogue to work simultaneously "above" and "below" the surface, which is absolutely essential for policy making. Similarly, introjection is defined as what the group internalizes (e.g., "decides" to own) from what is projected onto it. Introjection can lead a group to act upon what the rest of society projects onto it.

A schematic representation of the Socio-Analytic Map of the Country is shown at the end of the Appendix.

SEQUENCING PRINCIPLES

The idea that psychosocial dynamics can divert policies from their objectives is completely absent from public policy debates. The idea that policies can become social defenses is one of the main contributions of Socio-Analytic Dialogue. This is different from most psychological aspects taken into account in public policy since social defenses are mostly unconscious.

First Sequencing Principle:

> For each anxiety, resulting in a lack of sufficient containment, social defenses will be activated sequentially, until one is found capable to address it sufficiently well.

Social defenses are likely to be of an increasingly regressed nature. With public policy, defenses—unlike the case in the analytic dyad—are mobilized sequentially. Furthermore, psychosocial transmission mechanisms can lead policies to fail.

Second Sequencing Principle:

> Once basic needs are met, policies that can potentially satisfy social defense needs will be used for that purpose first, and it is only once the components of a policy that can be used as social defenses have been mobilized for that purpose that agents will be able to allow the policy to work towards achieving its stated objectives.

Policy makers and their constituents may not even be aware of what leads to a policy being derailed since a large share of the psychosocial mechanisms involved are unconscious.

ANALYTICAL ATTITUDE AT THE COUNTRY LEVEL

The idea of structural change at any given level of a society is widely used in policy making. However, it only refers to "above" the surface observed changes in economics, social, or lifestyle issues. The important psychoanalytic notion of therapeutic action can also be extended at the country level by defining it as the increased ability of a society to reflect on psychosocial issues that may be hampering its ability to implement the structural changes that it has chosen for itself (e.g., difficulty in group mourning, dealing with anxieties, nature of inter-groups projections and introjections, nature of social defenses used).

Empathic availability also plays a prominent role in country level policy making. Psychoanalysis emphasizes the feelings of togetherness and shared meaning which empathic availability can bring to communication. Although expressed in the context of the analytic dyad, the exact same words could have been written in the burgeoning economic development literature on internalization and ownership of reforms. Although radical shifts in internalization and ownership can sometimes appear to be the result of a sudden transformation, they are, however, almost systematically, the results of long and sometimes acrimonious processes.

The fundamental premise of Socio-Analytic Dialogue is that it may be possible to facilitate these shifts through psychosocial interventions piloted by the countries themselves. This requires that sufficient attention be paid to the complexities of each country. These are determined by that country's history, in particular its traumas, and its culture. Focusing on inter-group projections and introjections that exist can often disentangle these complexities. The various projections will often presage conflicts and resistance to change; subgroups' mental representations of others an ideal place to begin understanding how history and culture have left their mark on a society. As such, these mental representations must not only be understood but also, as indicators of existing or future splits in the society, be empathically communicated to others.

The Analytic Attitude at the Country Level is defined as follows:

> Unrestricted willingness and ability to temporarily experience, in order to be able to communicate them to others, each of the inter-groups' projections and introjections as if they were our own.

Psychosocially-informed listening and empathic availability at a societal level can increase the ability of policy makers to: (i) understand subgroups' affects and their psychosocial consequences; (ii) communicate with the various subgroups; (iii) have the credibility to question the validity of existing projections and introjections; and (iv) potentially improve society's collective ability to address subgroups' affects and their consequences.

POLICIES IN THE AGE OF CONTEMPT

Perverse societal dynamics are one of the single most important sources of anxieties worldwide. They can adversely impact public policies and limit a society's ability to provide a safe psychological environment.

The social defenses mobilized in response to anxieties are a function of the country romance (e.g., shared narratives). Although a psychosocial concept, shared narratives have already been incorporated into public policy thinking since they are at the foundation of Identity Economics applied to macroeconomics. See, Akerlof and Schiller (2009).

The specificity of the framework is due to the fact that it explicitly differentiates between two sources of anxieties: structural changes in the environment; and perverse societal dynamics.

One of the main tasks of Socio-Analytic Dialogue is to identify anxieties, be they existing or induced by a policy. First, there are anxieties induced by structural changes in the environment. An example is the decrease in connectedness between individuals due to the increased preponderance of transaction-driven instrumental relationships. Connectedness' gradual disappearance is often experienced as destroying society's ability to perform its containing function. In response, individuals may feel that their identity is under threat and react accordingly. This, in turn, becomes one of the most important psychosocial mechanisms leading a society to mobilize regressed collective defenses.

Second, there are anxieties induced by perverse societal dynamics. In a perverse social system, individuals are often treated with contempt and denigrated as they are used instrumentally to satisfy the needs of others. See, Long (2008). Anxieties stemming from being denigrated, meaning subject to repeated narcissistic injuries, are of a different nature than those stemming from structural changes in the environment. While the latter are perceived as affecting everyone in the same way, anxieties induced by perverse societal dynamics, because they only affect specific subgroups, are often experienced as personal attacks. As such, the social defenses mobilized to fend them off, including rejection of the perverse dynamics themselves, can have a sudden and significant impact on policies. Once group revulsion at perverse dynamics reaches a certain threshold, social defenses may become drastically altered as groups deliberately choose to abandon the system. This is called "Exit."

In several countries, a significant share of the population experiences the society as unfair and dysfunctional. Whether these individuals decide to react and, if so, how can vary greatly. For example, "Exit" can signify a forced breakdown of the system through mass protests, a retreat away from it with symptoms such as disillusionment or enactments of potentially dangerous fantasies. Regardless, "Exit" is likely to have a significant impact on social defenses and, therefore, on policies. As such, the "Policies in the Age of Contempt" framework is useful to structure thoughts about psychosocial dynamics and policies in a world where perverse societal dynamics dominate.

A schematic presentation of the framework is shown at the end of the Appendix.

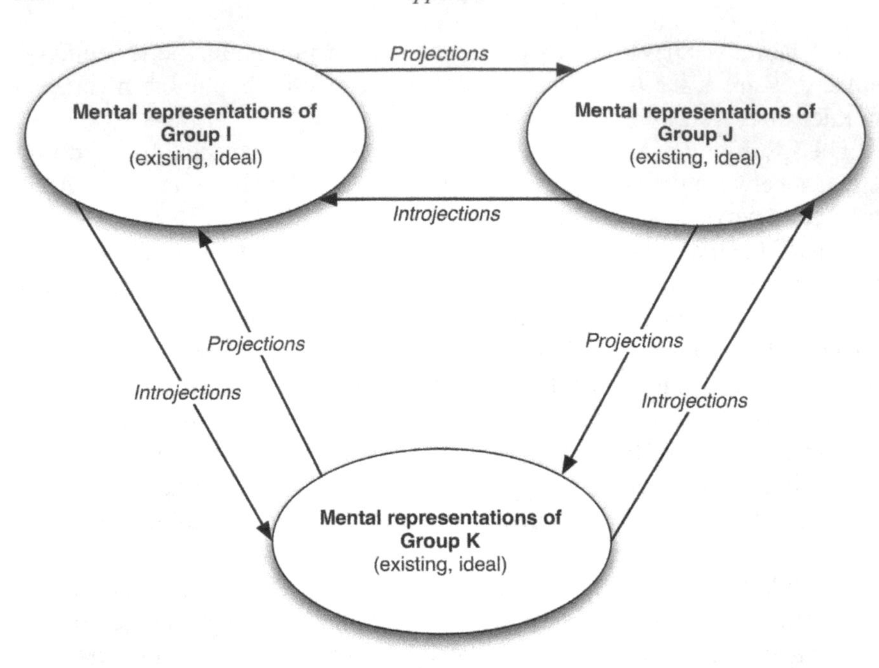

Figure A.1. Socio-Analytic Map of the Country. *www.socioanalyticdialogue.org*

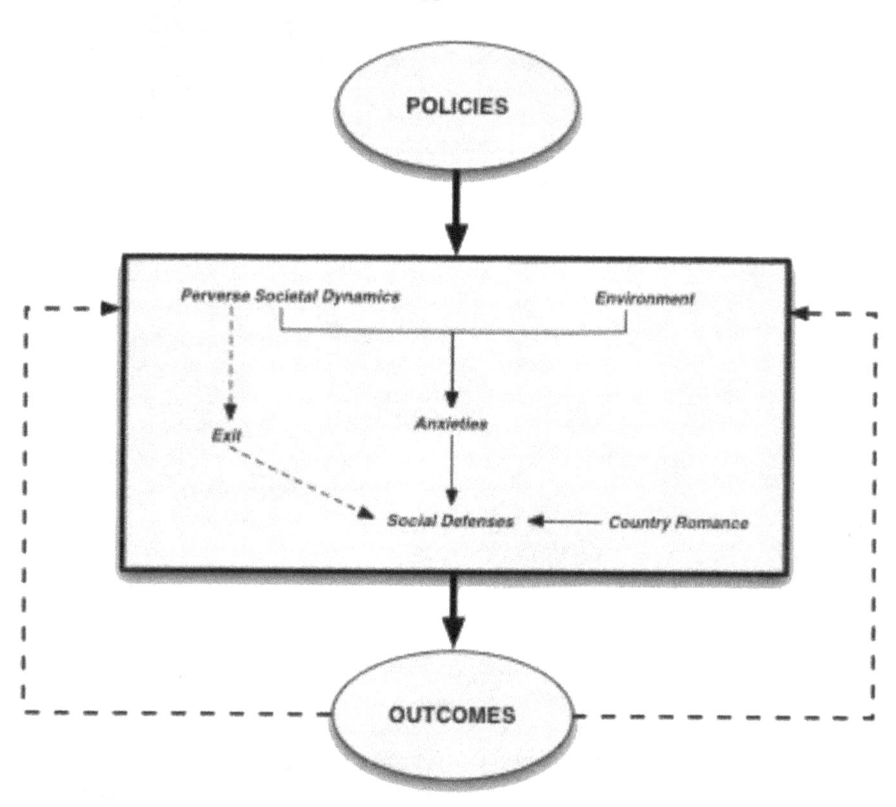

Figure A.2. Policies in the Age of Contempt. *www.socioanalyticdialogue.org*

Bibliography

Akerlof, George, and Robert Shiller. *Animal Spirits: How Human Psychology Drives the Economy and Why it Matters for Global Capitalism*. Princeton, New Jersey: Princeton University Press, 2009.

Armstrong, David and Michael Rustin (editors). *Social Defenses against Anxieties: Exploration in a Paradigm*. London: Routledge 2014.

Atlantic Currents. "The Covid-19 crisis viewed from the South," *Atlantic Currents*, Policy Center for the New South, Rabat, (2021).

Ben Smaïl, Nedra, and Bruno Boccara. "You only Die Once: Why not Make it Martyrdom," *Bulletin of the Psychoanalytic Association of New York*, Vol. 53, No. 1, (Spring 2015).

Bergholtz, Emil, Nele Brusselaers, and Andrew Ewing. "Global tipping points: Climate Change and the new coronavirus," *Politico*, January 5, 2022, https://www.politico.eu/article/climate-change-coronavirus-global-tipping-points/.

Boccara, B. "Socioanalytic dialogue," Chapter 14 of Long, S. *Socioanalytic Methods*, London: Karnac Books, 2013a.

Boccara, Bruno. *Bolivia: revirtiendo traumas*. La Paz, Bolivia: Ediciones Plural, 2013b.

Boccara, Bruno. *Socio-Analytic Dialogue: Incorporating Psychosocial Dynamics into Public Policies*, Lanham, Maryland: Lexington Books, 2014.

Han, Byung-Chul. *Psycho-politics: neo-liberalism and new technologies of power*. London: Verso Books, 2017.

Harari, Yuval Noah. "The world after coronavirus," *Financial Times*, March 20, 2020.

Hoggett, Paul, Wendy Hollway, Chris Robertson and Sally Weintrobe. *Climate Psychology: A Matter of Life and Death*. Phoenix Pub House, 2022.

Johanssen, Jacob. "Social Media in Times of Coronavirus: A Paranoid-Schizoid Pandemic," *Human Arenas*, Vol. 4, 2021.

Kolbert, Elizabeth. *The Sixth Extinction: An Unnatural History*. New York: Henry Holt, 2014.

Lacan, Jacques. Encore. *The Seminars of Jacques Lacan*. Book 20 1972–73. New York: W.W. Norton, 1998.

Lasch, Christopher. *The Culture of Narcissism*. New York: W. W. Norton, 1979.

Long, Susan. *The Perverse Organization and its Deadly Sins*. London: Karnac Books, 2008.

Long, Susan. *Socioanalytic Methods*. London: Karnac Books, 2013.
Long, Susan. "Turning a Blind Eye to Climate Change," *Organisational and Social Dynamics*, Vol. 15, No. 2, 2015.
Long, Susan. "Repairing the damage: wishful, defensive, or restorative," *Organisational and Social Dynamics*, Vol. 21, No. 1, 2021.
Ludwig, Mike. "Before 2001invasion, Bush Admin Declared Taliban an Ally in the War on Drugs." *Truthout*, August 19, 2021, https://truthout.org/articles/before-2001-invasion-bush-admin-declared-taliban-an-ally-in-the-war-on-drugs/?utm_campaign=Truthout+Share+Buttons&fbclid=IwAR2wwe0cvEiIeFxuk1qeqmvu1sspxgqMPGLappr3zUAuDSjVHNMe6UTHnrg.
Manukyan, Suren. "The World Will Never Be The Same Again." *EVN Report*, April 21, 2020, https://evnreport.com/covid-19/the-world-will-never-be-the-same-again/.
Mesa Gisbert, Carlos. *Presidencia Sitiada*. La Paz, Bolivia: Plural Editores, 2008.
Perlroth, Nicole. *This is how they tell me the world ends: The Cyber Weapons Arms Race*. New York: Bloomsbury Publishing, 2021.
Reister, Helmut. "Impfen macht frei—Parole: Justiz jagt Corona-Leugner." *Abendzeitung*, October 29, 2021, https://www.abendzeitung-muenchen.de/muenchen/impfen-macht-frei-parole-justiz-jagt-corona-leugner-art-766971.
Rosa, Hartmut. "We can quit the rat race." Interview given at University of Jena, April 3, 2020, https://www.uni-jena.de/en/200403_Rosa_Interview.
Scharff, David. *Object Relations, Theory and Practice*, Oxford, United Kingdom: Rowman and Littlefield, 1996.
Shapiro, Edward. *Finding a Place to Stand: Developing Self-Reflective Institutions, Leaders, and Citizens*, Oxford, United Kingdom, Phoenix Publishing House, 2019.
Slaby, Michael. "How we choose to recover will set the tone for the next century." *Medium*, May 8, 2020, https://medium.com/@slaby/how-we-choose-to-recover-will-set-the-tone-for-the-next-century-15eddae052d6.
Stapley, Lionel. *Globalization and Terrorism*. London: Karnac Books, 2006.
Turkle, Sherry. *Alone Together*. New York: Basic Books, 2011.
United Nations Independent Panel for Pandemic Preparedness and Response. *Covid-19: Make it the Last Pandemic*. New York: United Nations, 2021.
Volkan, Vamik. *Killing in the Name of Identity*. Durham, North Carolina: Pitchstone Publishing, 2006.
Volkan, Vamik. *Blood Lines: from ethnic pride to ethnic terrorism*. Boulder, Colorado: Westview Press, 1997.

Index

Printed in the USA
CPSIA information can be obtained
at www.ICGtesting.com
LVHW040545201023
761597LV00011B/1069

9 780761 873563